THE BLACK ROOTS AND WHITE RACISM OF EARLY PENTECOSTALISM IN THE USA

The Black Roots and White Racism of Early Pentecostalism in the USA

Iain MacRobert

Foreword by
Walter J. Hollenweger

MACMILLAN
PRESS

First published 1988

Published by
THE MACMILLAN PRESS LTD
Houndmills, Basingstoke, Hampshire RG21 2XS
and London
Companies and representatives
throughout the world

British Library Cataloguing in Publication Data
MacRobert, Iain
The black roots and white racism of
early pentecostalism in the USA.
1. Pentecostalism—United States—
History
I. Title
277.3′082   BR1644.5.U6
ISBN 978-1-349-19490-2   ISBN 978-1-349-19488-9 (eBook)
DOI 10.1007/978-1-349-19488-9

For My Brothers and Sisters of the African
Diaspora

Contents

Preface

This book is an unforseen consequence of research, which I began in 1981, into the reasons for the non-integration of the black-led and white-led Pentecostal congregations in England. Increasingly my narrow parochial study became something of a historical and geographical odyssey as the realisation grew that many of the profound differences which underly the superficial similarities in the black and white Pentecostal churches are a legacy from the bi-cultural crucible of the New World in which the Pentecostal movement was born and grew and fragmented during the early years of this century.

However, my 'journey' in time and space was not to end in the Americas of the early 1900s, for the black Christian tradition from which the Pentecostal movement sprang still possessed something of that spiritual heritage from West Africa, which had survived the aculturising and dehumanising brutality of the Middle Passage and slavery, and sustained black Christians during that long dark night of bondage and the grey dawn of an emancipation which continued to deny black people equality with whites.

Among the many people who have been of assistance I would especially like to thank my Pentecostal friends – both black and white – for sharing their experiences and understandings with me; the library staff at the Oldbury building of Sandwell College of Further and Higher Education for their invaluable help in obtaining books and papers; Professor Walter Hollenweger of Birmingham University for his encouragement and the loan of books from his personal collection; Rev Roswith Gerloff and Rev Dr Bongani Mazibuko for their assurances that my perceptions were shared by others; Tony Martin for reading the final draft and ensuring that my idiosyncratic style did not depart too much from standard English; and my wife Janet who, in addition to producing the typescript, has been both my severest critic and my most strenuous supporter.

The author and publishers wish to thank the following who have kindly given permission for the use of copyright material: Wm B.

Eerdmans Publishing Co., for the extracts from Vinson Synan, *The Holiness–Pentecostal Movement in the United States*; Gayroud S. Wilmore, for the extracts from his book *Black Religion and Black Radicalism* (originally published in 1972 by Doubleday; 2nd edn by Orbis Books in 1982); Oxford University Press, for the extracts from Robert M. Anderson, *Vision of the Disinherited: the Making of American Pentecostalism* and from Albert J. Rabotean. *Slave Religion: the Invisible Institution in the Antebellum South*; and Douglas J. Nelson, for the extracts from his Ph.D. dissertation *For Such a Time as This: the Story of Bishop William J. Seymour and the Azusa Street Revival*.

Every effort has been made to trace all the copyright holders but if any have been inadvertently overlooked the author and publishers would be pleased to make the necessary arrangement at the first opportunity.

Langley   IAIN MACROBERT

Foreword: Pentecostalism: Promises and Problems

Why is it that a country like Britain with its long tradition of democracy and human rights and some of the best anti-racism laws in the world, is experiencing racial tensions and race riots? Why is it that, although there is no legal apartheid here, there is a *de facto* exclusion of black people from higher education, from the police, from politics and, alas, also from office in the mainline churches?

The usual explanation given is: Blacks do not present themselves as police recruits, as university students, or as candidates for the ministry.

This is an all too facile explanation. 'Blacks do not want to become, pastors', it is said. Why is it then that the Birmingham area has 120 independent black congregations, complete with their pastors, bishops and many of them with their own church buildings?

At the university the situation is similar. No one can convince me that out of the thousands of young black people in Britain almost no one is intelligent enough to study at a British university. But, looking at our student body, one could get this impression. It is a false impression. The Centre for Black and White Christian Partnership is proof to the contrary. It is said that blacks do not want to study. Why then is it that this Centre (which was started with the help of a South African and a German doctoral student) year after year attracts many black students to spend their weekends working for a Certificate in Theology at the University of Birmingham?

Since I do not believe that the reason for racial tension in Britain is ill-will or blatant racism, one must look for another explanation. Especially important is the church scene, for the behaviour of the churches is in stark contradiction to their message. What could be the reason for this?

I believe that Iain MacRobert's book goes far to explain the root cause for the division between black and white churches in general and black and white Pentecostal churches in particular.

His explanation is also applicable to the tensions between black and white Christians in mainline churches.

MacRobert shows an alternative to the way we deal with the race problem. The alternative is the early Pentecostal church. Not only did black and white meet in early Pentecostalism, but the meeting between black and white was at the root of the worldwide revival called Pentecostalism. MacRobert is especially interested in the black component of this encounter. He shows that the structure of black slave religion, including some of their thought-patterns from their African past, were not only the reason for their survival in a hostile environment but also responsible for the success of early Pentecostalism. Since the early Christian church had many slaves amongst its early converts and since these slaves belonged to an oral culture, it is not astonishing that there are parallels between, for instance, Corinthian Christianity and early Pentecostal Christianity.

However, in the racial climate of the United States at the beginning of our century, such an inter-racial spirituality was considered to be 'unchristian' and 'immoral'. It was not acceptable to the mainline churches that a black evangelist from Louisiana could teach them anything.

Black spirituality in Pentecostalism is evidenced by scores of black hymn-writers and evangelists and above all by William J. Seymour (1870–1922), a son of former slaves from Centerville, Louisiana. Seymour taught himself to read and write and was for a time a student in Charles Fox Parham's Pentecostal Bible School in Topeka, Kansas. Parham (1873–1929), often described as a pioneer of pentecostalism, was also a sympathiser of the Ku Klux Klan and therefore he excluded Seymour from his Bible classes. Seymour was allowed only to listen outside the classroom through the half-open door.

In the face of constant humilitation, Seymour became an apostle of reconciliation. He developed a spirituality that in 1906 led to the revival in Los Angeles which most Pentecostal historians believe to be the cradle of Pentecostalism. 'It may be categorically stated that black pentecostalism emerged out of the context of the brokenness of black existence', writes black pentecostal historian Leonad Lovett.[1]

MacRobert describes in detail the roots of Seymour's spirituality which lay in the African and Afro–American past of his people, in their experience of spirits, in their dehumanisation and liberation, in their songs, in the way they told the stories of the Bible as their story. Seymour affirmed his black heritage by introducing Negro spirituals and Negro music into his liturgy at a time when this music was considered inferior and unfit for Christian worship, for he had drunk from 'the "invisible institution" of black folk Christianity' with its themes of freedom, equality and community.[2]

In the revival in Los Angeles, white bishops and black workers, men and women, Asians and Mexicans, white professors and black laundry women came together as equals (1906!). 'Proud well-dressed preachers came to "investigate". Soon their high looks were replaced with wonder, then conviction comes, and very often you will find them in a short time wallowing on the dirty floor, asking God to forgive them and make them as little children', we read in the first issue of Seymour's newspaper.[3] 'That the one outstanding personality in bringing about the Pentecostal revival in Los Angeles was a Negro in a fact of extreme importance to Pentecostals of all races', writes white Pentecostal historian Vinson Synan.[4]

No wonder that the religious and secular press reported the events in detail. As they could not understand the revolutionary nature of this Pentecostal spirituality, they took refuge in ridicule and scoffed, 'What good can come from a self-appointed Negro prophet?'

The mainline churches also criticised the early Pentecostal movement. They despised the Pentecostals because of their lowly black origins. This social pressure soon prompted the emerging Pentecostal church bureaucracy to tame the Los Angeles revival. Pentecostal churches segregated into black and white organisations just as most of the other churches had done.

The black churches developed an oral liturgy, a narrative theology, and maximum participation at the levels of reflection and decision-making. They used dreams and visions as a form of iconography in their communities and expressed their understanding of the body/mind relationship in praying for the sick.

All this was, and still is, considered to be inferior to white Christianity. Yet it is not inferior. It is different. And it could become vital for white churches to recover some of the oral culture of our common past.

As to the *de facto* segregation into white and black Christianity in Britain, the reason now seems clear. They are two cultures, an

oral, narrative, inclusive black culture and a literary, conceptual, exclusive white culture. The two integrate very badly and
only if some of the black and white Christians become
'bilingual'.

As to white pentecostalism in Europe and America, it is now
fast developing into an evangelical middle-class religion. Many
of the elements that were vital for its rise and expansion in the
Third World are disappearing. They are being replaced by
efficient fund-raising structures, a streamlined ecclesiastical
bureaucracy and a Pentecostal conceptual theology – usually,
but not always, an Anglo-Saxon evangelicalism onto which is
tacked the doctrine of speaking in tongues as evidence of spirit
baptism. One has to agree with MacRobert's statement: 'To see
the Pentecostal movement simply in terms of a re-emergence of
glossolalic manifestations would be a grave error.'[5] Pentecost is
more than speaking in tongues, although one should not despise
the value of glossolalia as a form of 'prayer without making
grammatical sentences', a kind of socio-acoustic sanctuary for
people who do not have and do not need cathedrals, a form of
psycho-hygienic worship experience which deals with the fears
and frustrations, the joys and hopes buried deep in our
unconsciousness, or in the words of Paul, a means 'to become a
more mature human being'.[6]

But there is more than this to Pentecost. Pentecost is an
intercultural agent throwing a bridge across the troubled waters
between two cultures which otherwise may never meet.

With his story MacRobert has not only given us a brilliant
piece of historical research, but also focused our attention on
aspects of our common heritage which we have ignored but
which are vital for our survival.

University of Birmingham   WALTER J. HOLLENWEGER

The Spirit

In the last days, God says, I will pour out my Spirit on all people. Your sons and daughters will prophecy, your young men will see visions, your old men will dream dreams. Even on my servants, both men and women, I will pour out my Spirit in those days, and they will prophecy.

St. Peter quoting the Prophet Joel

No man can genuinely experience the fullness of the Spirit and remain a bona fide racist.

Leonard Lovett

The Wall

Jesus Christ . . . is our peace, who has made the two one and has destroyed the barrier, the dividing wall of hostility.

St Paul

Your slaves will go to heaven if you are good, but don't ever think that you will be close to your mistress and master. No! No! there will be a wall between you; but there will be holes in it that will permit you to look out and see your mistress when she passes by. If you want to sit behind this wall, you must do the language of the text 'Obey your masters'.

Frank Roberson, a paraphrase of the type of sermon which he and other slaves were subjected to

Pentecost is that event which broke down the walls of the nations, colour, language, sex and social class.

Walter J. Hollenweger

Introduction

The Pentecostal movement, which began at the start of the present century, is attracting increasing attention from scholars in many disciplines. Henry Pitt van Dusen, President emeritus of Union Theological Seminary in New York, has described it as the largest group within 'the Third Force in Christendom', alongside the first and second forces of Roman Catholicism and Protestantism.[1] He wrote:

> When historians of the future come to assess the most significant development in Christendom in the first half of the 20th century, they will fasten on the ecumenical movement . . . but next to this they will decide that by all odds the most important fact in the Christian history of our times was a *New Reformation*, the emergence of a new, third major type and branch of Christendom, alongside of and not incommensurable with Roman Catholicism and historic Protestantism . . .[2]

Bishop Lesley Newbigin has described the Pentecostal movement as possessing 'the Third Ecclesiology' alongside the first ecclesiology of Roman Catholicism which emphasises sacramental participation, and the second ecclesiology of Protestantism which stresses the hearing of the gospel with faith. The third ecclesiology of the Pentecostals involves individuals being incorporated into the Church by receiving the abiding presence of the Holy Spirit. This somewhat narrow and inadequate definition of Pentecostalism nevertheless suggests that the historic denominations are beginning – albeit somewhat belatedly – to recognise that a new force is shaping the Church of the present and of the future.

This growing interest in the Pentecostal movement is fairly recent and to a great extent thrust upon the ecclesiastical and academic communities by its phenomenal growth, particularly in the countries of the third world. Professor Walter J. Hollenweger – himself a former Pentecostal pastor – writes:

> Thus when in Chile, Brazil and other countries it has more adherents than all other Protestants, when in France and Russia, Nigeria and South Africa it is far and away the most

1

rapidly growing religious group, and when even the intellec-
tuals of Europe and America rediscover with its aid long
buried levels of human existence, it is not surprising that
Roman Catholic theologians and sociologists and even atheist
anthropologists and experts in African studies are beginning
to take an interest in the phenomenon.[3]

In the future, the historic churches and Christianity in general
will have to come to terms with a world in which most Christians
will probably be in the underdeveloped or developing nations,
most will be non-European and most will be of the Pentecostal
oral narrative type.[4] The Pentecostal's most distinctive and
universal characteristic is the central place they ascribe to the
influence of the Holy Spirit upon the individual and the Church.
The 'manifestation of the Spirit' most often associated with
Pentecostalism is speaking with tongues or glossolalia, which is
understood by most – but by no means all – Pentecostals as the
evidence of a person having received the Spirit baptism. Cyril G.
Williams, of the University of Wales, writes: '. . . never before in
the history of the whole Christian Church or in any part of it, has
glossolalia erupted with such vigour and in so widespread a
manner as in this century. It came to the fore as a central feature
in Pentecostalism . . .'[5] Yet to see the Pentecostal movement
simply in terms of a re-emergence of glossolalic manifestations
would be a grave error. The limitation of Spirit baptism to that
which is evidenced by glossolalia was a later rationalisation of
white Pentecostals. Most of the early Pentecostals, and to a great
extent the black Pentecostals in the United States, the
Caribbean and Britain today, are involved in a total experience
of the Spirit which transcends the limitations set by the white
Pentecostal denominations.

An adequate comprehension of black Pentecostalism, however, can only be derived from a study of the religion which
survived the middle passage in the hearts and minds of West
Africans and their descendants.[6] The black understanding and
practice of Christianity which developed in the crucible of New
World slavery was a syncretism of Western theology and West
African religious practice and beliefs. The African diaspora often
manifested an outward commitment to Western Christianity but
beneath this persona, to a greater or lesser extent, an African
heart continued to pulsate with black longings, black ambitions

and a black spirituality which integrated the seen and unseen worlds, which made no distinction between sacred and profane, which opened up the black person to God and brought the power of the divine into the concrete realities of racist America.

The birth in 1906 of the Pentecostal movement owes much to this black syncretised Christianity and to black spirituality. In fact, it may be argued with some justification, that there would be no worldwide Pentecostal or Charismatic movements if it were not for their 'black roots', which Hollenweger has summarised as:

1. orality of liturgy;
2. narrativity of theology and witness;
3. maximum participation at the levels of reflection, prayer and decision-making and therefore a form of community which is reconciliatory;
4. inclusion of dreams and visions into personal and public forms of worship; they function as kinds of icons for the individual and the community;
5. an understanding of the body/mind relationship which is informed by experiences of correspondence between body and mind; the most striking application of this insight is the ministry of healing by prayer.[7]

In this volume I have attempted to outline the origins of Pentecostalism: its West African heritage, its roots in American slave religion and the Wesleyan–Holiness movement, its birth in 1906 at the Azusa Street Mission in Los Angeles and its subsequent division on the basis of race.

1 Some Glossolalic Precursors of the Pentecostal Movement

> And when the day of Pentecost was fully come, they were all with one accord in one place. And suddenly there came a sound from heaven as of a rushing mighty wind, and it filled all the house where there were sitting. And there appeared unto them cloven tongues like as of fire, and it sat upon each of them. And they were all filled with the Holy Ghost, and began to speak with other tongues, as the Spirit gave them utterance.
>
> Acts 2:1–4, KJV

The twentieth-century Pentecostal movement claims to have returned to the doctrines, experiences and practices of the Apostolic Church of the first century and, in particular, Pentecostals speak of having received the same powerful, miraculous, pneumatic experience as the early Church.

The first issue of William J. Seymour's 'Apostolic Faith' newspaper which dates from the beginning of the Pentecostal movement in September 1906, states that: 'The Baptism with the Holy Ghost is a gift of power on the sanctified life; so when we get it it we have the same evidence as the Disciples received on the Day of Pentecost, in speaking in new tongues.'[1]

Not all Pentecostals accept glossolalia as the only initial evidence of a person having received the Spirit baptism. For example, one of the 'Fundamental Beliefs' of the Elim Pentecostal Church in Britain is: 'We believe that our Lord Jesus Christ is the Baptiser in the Holy Ghost and that this Baptism with signs following is promised to every believer.'[2] However, the majority of Pentecostals in Britain and the United States maintain that glossolalia is both the evidence of Spirit Baptism and a distinctive characteristic of Pentecostalism. T. B. Barratt, the British born Pentecostal pioneer in Norway, stated that what made the Pentecostal movement distinctive was its: '... definite claim to be baptised in the Holy Ghost in the same way as the one hundred and twenty on the day of Pentecost, a Spirit baptism accompanied by the speaking in tongues ...'.[3] Similarly, Donald Gee who was one of the most respected and influential men in the British Pentecostal Assemblies of God, wrote: 'The particular and distinctive testimony of the Pentecostal Movement has been that the outward evidences that accompanied the baptism of the Holy Spirit in primitive christian experience can be, should be, and are being repeated up to date.' He went on to assert that: 'The most usual and most persistent manifesttion was speaking with tongues', and that, '... the Pentecostal Movement has consistently taught that speaking with tongues is the scriptural initial evidence of that baptism'.[4]

Similar sentiments form part of the statements of belief of most British and American Pentecostal organisations. For example, items eight and nine of the declaration of faith of the Church of God (Cleveland) state that they believe 'in the baptism of the Holy Ghost subsequent to a clean heart', and 'in speaking with other tongues as the Spirit gives utterance, and that it is the initial evidence of the baptism of the Holy Ghost'.[5]

Secular scholars have described the movement in similar terms. Robert Mapes Anderson declares that: 'Certainly, one may find in Pentecostalism elements of religion as dogma, ritual, ethics, social association and convention, but early Pentecostalism at least was first and foremost religion as emotional experience and expression'.[6]

The twentieth-century Pentecostal movement falls into that tradition of enthusiastic, ecstatic and experiential Christianity which has made brief appearances in Church history since the time of the Apostles.[7] Montanism, which originated as a reaction to ecclesiasticism around the second half of the second century AD, has been referred to as, 'the fountainhead of all the enthusiastic or pneumatic movements in Christian history'.[8] Frederick Dale Bruner states that there is a 'striking similarity at almost every point between the doctrinal and experiential emphasis of Montanism and those of modern Pentecostalism'.[9] Quoting from Seeberg, he summarises the essential character of Montanism as follows:

1. The last period of revelation has opened. It is the day of spiritual gifts. The recognition of spiritual 'charismata' is a distinguishing trait of Montanism. This involves primarily the acknowledgement of the Paraclete ...

2. The orthodoxy of the Montanists is acknowledged – their acceptance of the rules of faith. The Monarchianism in utterances of Montanus is due to lack of theological culture ...
3. The nearness of the end of the world is strongly emphasised.
4. There are strict moral requirements.[10]

Similarly, the twentieth century Pentecostal movement believe that:

1. the final period of revelation has begun with the outpouring of the 'latter rain' – the 'baptism of the Holy Spirit' – and the return of spiritual gifts to the church.
2. most Pentecostals are considered orthodox in belief, except for their distinctive doctrine of the Holy Spirit, which, however, is no more 'unorthodox' than one of its major precursors: the Wesleyan doctrine of sanctification. One of the less orthodox branches of the Movement espouse a form of modalism which they term 'Oneness'. However, neither the Oneness Pentecostals nor those who adhere to the doctrine of the trinity appear to have much understanding of the trinitarian creeds or of the controversies which engendered them.[11]
3. The imminent physical return of Christ to set up a millennial kingdom is expected.
4. there are generally strict moral standards and a rigorous system of personal ethics and taboos.

Since the Montanists, a number of groups and individuals have followed in this ecstatic tradition, though by no means all of them have practised glossolalia.[12] Among those who have, were the French Jansenists in 1731, and earlier, in the late seventeenth century, the Camisards or French Prophets of south eastern France who, when forced to flee from persecution, had some success in England and influenced a group of Quakers – later called Shakers – in Manchester.[13] Their most prominent leader, 'Mother' Ann Lee, after being tried for heresy, left England and travelled to America with a group of fellow Shakers in 1774.[14] There they founded a communitarian settlement from whence evangelistic endeavours and the revivalism of the 1830s led to the establishment of ecstatic Shaker communities throughout the north east United States by the mid 19th century.[15]

Around the same time there were outbursts of glossolalia in

Scandinavian revivals; the influence of the glossolalic followers of the Scottish ex-Presbyterian, Edward Irving, led to the establishment, of 'Catholic Apostolic Church' congregations in Britain and the United States; Mormonism came into being with claims of spiritual gifts which included glossolalia;[16] and the Millerites, and one group of New England Adventists known as the 'Gift People' also practised speaking in tongues.[17] The latter held their first national convention in 1875, and it was reported that 'thousands' came to see 'the marvellous works of the Holy Spirit; many messages were given in unknown tongues; some were slain and baptised in the Holy Spirit – it was Pentecost indeed'. Beginning in 1886, annual conventions were held at Ashdod near West Duxbury, Massachusetts. One such convention was in progress in April 1906 when the Pentecostal Movement was being brought to birth in Los Angeles.[18]

In Los Angeles itself, another glossolalic group which had originated about the middle of the nineteenth century in Southern Russia and Armenia, were drawn to the Azusa Street Mission of the black Holiness preacher, William Joseph Seymour, by the discovery that others now shared their experienced of speaking in tongues.[19]

It is to Azusa that we must look for the birthplace of twentieth century Pentecostalism, for as Vinson Synan says: 'Directly or indirectly, practically all of the Pentecostal groups in existence can trace their lineage to the Azusa Mission.'[20] Furthermore, as Leonard Lovett has made clear, because the movement was brought to birth in an all black prayer meeting: 'One cannot meaningfully discuss the origins of contemporary pentecostalism unless the role of blacks is clearly defined and acknowledged.'[21]

2 The Roots of Pentecostalism: Black American Christianity

Weigh well these my words ... the decree hath already passed the judgement seat of an UNDEVIATING God, wherein he hath said, 'surely the cries of the black, a most persecuted people, ascended to my throne and craved my mercy; now, behold! I will stretch forth mine hand and gather them to the palm, that they become unto me a people, and I unto them their God' ... learn, slave holder thine will rests not in thine hand: God decrees to thy slave his rights as a man.

Robert Alexander Young, *The Ethiopian Manifesto*

It may be categorically stated that black Pentecostalism emerged out of the context of the brokenness of black existence.... Their holistic view of religion had its roots in African religion.

Leonard Lovett

Elements in the religion of Seymour, of other black Americans, and of West Indian Pentecostals, including those now settled in Britain, cannot be fully understood without some consideration of their African origins and the conditions of slavery under which a black understanding of Christianity was formed.

The process of stripping the slaves of most of their culture was remarkably rapid. It began with the dehumanising conditions in which they were held in Africa and then shipped to the markets of the New World without regard to differences of sex, age, family or tribe. This process continued on the farms and plantations of America and the West Indies where they came under the strict discipline and relentless supervision of their white owners or overseers. In particular, any attempt to retain and use their native languages was discouraged or prohibited, and slaves with the same mother tongue were generally kept apart.

The conditions of slavery, and in particular the forced

mobility of slaves, all but destroyed social bonds, the African sense of community and the family. E. Franklin Frazier claims that this destruction of the forces of social cohesion included religion, and that: '. . . it is impossible to establish any continuity between African religious practises and the Negro church in the United States'.[1] However, other researchers such as Melville J. Herskovits (1958), Gayraud S. Wilmore (1972), James H. Cone (1972), Joseph R. Washington (1973), and Albert J. Raboteau (1978) have established that some continuity of belief and practice between African religion and black North American Christianity does exist.[2]

The religious beliefs or rituals of any people are to some degree determined by the material, social and psychological realities of life. For the slave, bondage, separation from homeland and the tyranny of the white slave master were formative in their adoption and adaptation of the Christian religion. The remnants of African religion and culture combined with the religion of the white man produced in the black American and West Indian what Wilmore has described as: 'something less and something more than what is generally regarded as the Christian religion'.[3]

Black people rejected the European distortion of Christianity which generally supported slavery and segregation, and took up a Christian faith with which they could identify through their sufferings and their desire for human dignity and freedom.[4]

Wilmore writes concerning the Christianity of the slaves:

> It was born in Blackness. Its most direct antecedents were the quasi-religious, quasi-secular meetings which took place on the plantations, unimpeded by white supervision and under the inspired leadership of the first generation of African priests to be taken in slavery. It was soon suppressed and dominated by the religious instruction of the Society for the Propagation of the Gospel in Foreign Parts and the colonial churches – especially the Baptists and Methodists. But the faith that evolved from the coming together of diverse religious influences was a 'tertium quid', distinctly different from its two major contributors.[5]

Similarly, Raboteau acknowledged that:

> Shaped and modified by a new environment, elements of

African folklore, music, language, and religion were trans-
planted to the New World by the African diaspora.... One of
the most durable and adaptable constituents of the slave's
culture, linking African past with American present, was his
religion. It is important to realise, however, that in the
Americas the religions of Africa have not been merely
preserved as static 'Africanisms' or as archaic 'retentions' ...
African styles of worship, forms of ritual, systems of belief, and
fundamental perspectives have remained vital on this side of
the Atlantic, not because they were preserved in a 'pure'
orthodoxy but because they were transformed. Adaptability,
based upon respect for spiritual power wherever it originated,
accounted for the openness of African religions to syncretism
with other religious traditions and for the continuity of a
distinctively African religious consciousness.[6]

James H. Cone maintains:

Many slaves ... merely pretended to accept white christianity
while actually holding quite different views. The slaves were
obliged to create their own religion out of the remnants that
were available and useful, both African and Christian.[7]

And Joseph R. Washington writes that:

The religion or 'cult' of black folk emerged in the crucible of
culture clashes – in the squeeze put on traditions of Africa by
those of the dominant New World ... black folk religion ...
(is) an emergent from traditional African religions, Western
civilization, and Christianity.[8]

AFRICAN RELIGIOUS ROOTS

Although a few of the Negroes brought as slaves from sub-
Saharan West Africa to the New World had been influenced by
Islam, or to a lesser extent by Christianity, the majority held to
the complex and sophisticated indigenous primal African
religious beliefs and ethics which they carried with them into
slavery.

The African primal folk religion of those taken into slavery
had no written creeds, written liturgies or holy books. It was
preliterate and passed on from generation to generation by oral

tradition and symbolism. It was in narratives – myths, legends and folk tales – riddles, songs, proverbs and other aphorisms that African theology was enshrined and codified. They were a means of preserving and transmitting knowledge, values, attitudes, morals, ethics, sacred rituals, dogma, history and the wisdom of the ancestors. These oral methods ensured the maintenance of social conformity and cultural continuity in Africa, and in the New World, elements of African cultural values, patterns of behaviour and religious beliefs and practises continued to be transmitted. African primal religion was danced and sung, beaten out in the rhythms and tones of 'talking' drums, the swaying of bodies and the stamping of feet, painted, cast in brass and carved in wood, ivory, clay and stone, enacted in ritual and drama.[9] Unlike Western Protestantism it was not individualistic but social; not so concerned with an individual's relationship with God as with the interrelationships between God, the spirits, the ancestors and the community: 'a person is only a human being in relation to other people.' African primal religion was anthropocentric and ontological. In Africa the ethnic community was the worshipping community and religion was concerned not simply with the 'soul' but with the whole of life and existence. Although there are more than a thousand black ethnolinguistic communities in Africa, and each has its own religious system there is a common world view:[10]

Wilmore states: 'The native religions of West and Central Africa had a single dominating characteristic ... a profound belief that both the individual and the community had a continuous involvement with the spirit world in the practical affairs of daily life.'[11] African primal religions integrate the seen and unseen world. The supernatural, sacred, metaphysical and spiritual are merged with and influence the natural, profane, physical and material.[12] In fact, in most of the languages of Africa there is no native word for religion because religion is all of life. Consequently, man – for his own sake and that of the community – must understand and be involved with the spirit world by means of sacrifice, divination and spirit possession.

Such beliefs were not, as maintained by some Western scholars, simply crude animistic superstitions, but a diffused monotheism. For above and beyond the veneration given to mediators – symbols of the deity, deceased ancestors, spirit beings and divinities – was an understanding of the unique, immortal, personal, invisible, omnipotent, omniscient, omnipresent 'Great Spirit' or 'High God' who is the 'Supreme Being', 'Creator', 'Father', 'Mother', 'King', Judge and Redeemer, both transcendent and immanent, holy and kind, the provider and healer of his people. Furthermore, although West Africans held to an amoral concept of spiritual power, they differentiated between the uses to which such power could be put: the 'good magic' of the 'medicine man' which included the medicinal use of herbs, the giving of advice and council, protection from evil forces, ritual cleansing, the sale of amulets and charms, divination and the interpretation of events, was distinct from the 'bad magic' of the 'conjurer' or 'witch doctor' who was both hated and feared for his malevolent powers.[13] The medicine man was the precursor of the slave 'exhorters' who became the first religious leaders among the black slave community. Raboteau summarises the fundamental beliefs widely shared by diverse West African societies:

> ... belief in a transcendent, benevolent God, creator and ultimate source of providence; belief in a number of immanent gods, to whom people must sacrifice in order to make life propitious; belief in the power of spirits animating things and nature to affect the welfare of people; belief in priests and others who were expert in practical knowledge of the gods and spirits: belief in spirit possession, in which gods, through their devotees, spoke to men.[14]

There were differences in belief and in emphasis but there was a common theologial perspective and world view.

In Africa, spiritual and politial power were all but identical, and African religion was primarily concerned with power, for without the power of the Spirit of God – the vital force – man is helpless. This has been described by Joseph Washington as a kind of fatalism. It is the realisation of man's impotence to influence human affairs which impels the African to attune himself to God, either directly or, more commonly, through a mediator. The experience of slavery confirmd this fatalism, for human effort was insufficient to overthrow the tyranny of their bondage. Slaves, however, did not despair or resign themselves to the situation. They came together in a worshipping community to seek for a power greater than that of the human perpetrators of slavery. In the words of Washington: '... the spirits of God, gods, and ancestors working together are considered the most powerful forces in the universe. In this respect Africans are power worshippers. They seek power in all things and respect power potential wherever it is made manifest'.[15]

Black folk religion has continued to reflect an African 'fatalistic' world view as it has been confronted by slavery prejudice, segregation, discrimination and inequality, and the inefficacy of black human effort to destroy these things. In a society where they were consistently pushed to the bottom no matter how hard they tried and regardless of how they sought to utilise the same secular political means as whites, the powerless black religionists attuned their minds, emotions and bodies to God and received power from on high.

For the African, the black slave and the black American or West Indian Pentecostal, religion is primarily about experiencing the power of God. God's presence and power must be felt or revealed in a pragmatic, personal, subjective and even exciting way. It is a religion of the Spirit, and only in a secondary sense a religion of the Book. The Bible was often rejected by slaves because it was used by some white preachers to justify and uphold slavery.[16] The God they served in their secret meetings was a God who possessed them with his Spirit and liberated them in ecstatic worship. Within the bondage and sorrow of slavery there was a liberty and joy of relationship with the Spirit. Feelings, both of sorrow and joy, were to be experienced to the full, and were expressed in the melancholy and pathos of Negro spirituals, and in the shout, the song and the dance of excited worship and the celebration of life.[17]

One of the most distinctive elements of African primal religion to be manifest among the slaves of the New world, was the extensive use of music and rhythm. For the people of West Africa, drumming, singing, dancing and other motor behaviour is associated with rituals whereby devotees are possessed by lesser deities and spirits. Raboteau states that: 'So essential are music and dance to West African religious expression that it is no exaggeration to call them "danced religions".'[18] African music with its polyrhythmic character, percussive emphasis and heterophony, in conjunction with African dance, had religious and moral significance and was the living embodiment of African history. Dance was also associated with spirit possession in the same way as it was often linked to 'getting the Spirit' among Christian slaves and still is among many black Pentecostals today. [19]

In West Africa, tribal folk religion was pragmatic and adept at syncretising elements from the religions of other tribes and at adopting new gods, particularly when they were considered to be more powerful than their own. In the New World the protecting gods of Africa and the Supreme Being gradually became identified with saints, angels, demons and the God of the Bible, but black Christians retained their sense of community and rejected the passivity of missionary teaching which encouraged them to accept the dehumanising conditions imposed upon them by the white slave masters.

The religion of slavery was initially an adaption of African Abosom, Alose, Orisha, Vodun worship or 'Voodooism' which later overlaid with a veneer of Christianity. Ultimately it became Christian, yet it retained many African elements. [20]

A white Presbyterian missionary wrote of the antinomianism he had found among the black slaves in the Southern States of America:

> True religion they are inclined to place in profession, in forms and ordinances, and in excited states of feeling. And true conversion, in dreams, visions, trances, voices – all bearing a perfect or striking resemblance to some form or type which has been handed down for generations, or which has been originated in the wild fancy of some religious teacher among them. [21]

Such religious beliefs and practises were not the result of slave idiosyncrasies but were part of their West African folk heritage.

MISSIONS TO SLAVES

The Protestant Missionaries, to an even greater extent than the Roman Catholics, saw no relationship between the 'animism', 'polytheism', 'idolatry', 'fetishism' and 'superstition' of African religion and the message of Christ. Accordingly, they sought to annihilate it. [22] Roman Catholic missions began work among the Negroes in the early sixteenth Century and there were also cases of Africans being introduced to Protestantism at about the same

time, but the first systematic mission to slaves was inaugurated
in 1701 by the English Society for the Propagation of the Gospel
in Foreign Parts.

During the early years, slavery was often justified as a means
of converting the heathen to Christianity. Later missionaries
often appealed to the profit motive in order to persuade slave
owners to allow their slaves to receive religious instruction.
Converted slaves, they argued, were easier to control. By the
end of the eighteenth century, black preachers began to be
licensed by denominations, although they were already recognised by their own people prior to this.[23]

Most, though by no means all, missionaries avoided the
theological and ethical inconsistencies between the Christian
Gospel and the practise of slavery, and by the mid 19th Century
several catechisms had been writen for slaves.[24] One of these
included the following questions and responses:

Q. What did God make you for?
A. To make a crop.
Q. What is the meaning of 'Thou shalt not commit adultery'?
A. To serve our heavenly Father, and our earthly master, obey
our overseer, and not steal anything.[25]

On the other hand, there were also white missionaries, as
early as the mid-eighteenth century, who opposed slavery and
even became implicated in slave plots and uprisings. A century
later many white abolitionists, particularly Quakers and
Methodists, were motivated by Christianity.[26]

Most early missionaries to the slaves sought to demythologise
their perceptions of the world and to encourage their passive
acceptance of slavery by giving them the hope of heaven.
However, there were some elements in the Bible which could be
interpreted in terms of African religion and thus provide a
continuity of belief and practice. The Scriptures speak of
miracles, the exorcism of demons, the defeat of Satan and the
granting of the Spirit's power to believers that they might do
such things. The work of the Holy Spirit in the believer 'could
readily be interpreted by the slave as identical with conjuration
and the Orisha-possession of his ancestral religion'.[27] Common
to both religious traditions were other beliefs, such as the
fatherhood of God; the creation; mankind's loss of paradise,
eternal life and direct communion with God; a personal devil;

substitutionary and expiatory sacrifice; the efficacy of prayer; life after death; judgement and reward or punishment.[28]

The distinctive form of black Christianity was forged under, and to some degree in response to, the dehumanising conditions of slavery. It was the religion of an oppressed and segregated people who, torn from their homes, were forced to come to terms with colour as an identifier of status and the brutality of forced labour. Not surprisingly, it emphasised freedom, human welfare and human dignity. Freedom from sin became easily associated with freedom to give oneself up to the Spirit in worship and, more importantly, with the longing for freedom from the white slave master. Cone states:

> Freedom, for black slaves, was not a theological idea about being delivered from the oppression of sin. It was a historical reality that had transcendent implications. Freedom meant the end of 'driber's dribin', and 'missus' Scoldin' – Roll, Jordan, roll.' It meant that there would be 'no more peck o' corn', 'no more driver's lash', 'No more pint o' salt', 'no more hundred lash,' and 'no more mistress's call for me, many thousand gone.'[29]

In the dehumanising conditions of slavery the black religionists readily perceived the work of 'bad magic' and the devil, and turned to 'de Lawd' for power – if not to immediately extricate him from his plight – at least to aid him in physical and mental survival and to set him free in the spirit.[30] For the slaves, the work of the devil was perceived not merely in the spiritual realm but also in the concrete realities of every-day life. Cone writes: 'Anyone who was not for the Kingdom, as present in the liberating work of Jesus, was automatically for Satan, who stood for enslavement.... His earthly representatives are slave holders, slave catchers and slave traders.'[31]

Moral and ethical strictures were frequently ignored in the light of the hypocrisy of white Christianity. The slaves recognised the gross inconsistency between the teaching they received about the loving and all-powerful God of the white man, and the reality of white indifference to their powerlessness and suffering. Furthermore, in African primal religion, ethics are not so much a matter of personal morality or righteousness as of refraining from anti-social activity. Consequently, black slaves took from the Christianity of the white man only those elements which related to daily experience, eased the burden of slavery, reflected the belief systems of Africa or could be used to affirm their right to freedom and dignity.[32]

REVIVALS AND SPLITS

The Great Awakening had a profound effect on the slave population of America and through its influence many were converted to Christianity. By the end of the eighteenth century, about one quarter of all the Methodists and Baptists in the South were black. At the beginning of the 19th Century the revivalist camp meetings of the Great Western Revival further swelled the ranks of the black converted. By stressing the conversion experience rather than religious instruction, Christianity was made more accessible to the illiterate and poorly educated, both black and white. It was experiential rather than intellectual religion, and a converted heart was of greater importance than a theological education. At the meetings, black slave converts could exhort not only their fellow slaves but also whites, and a few became the Pastors of racially mixed and even predominantly white congregations. However, the real importance of these early black preachers was that they became the leaders of their own Negro movement which developed the bicultural synthesis of black Christianity.[33] Raboteau writes:

> The powerful emotionalism, ecstatic behaviour, and congregational responses of the revival were amenable to the African religious heritage of the slaves, and forms of African dance and song remained in the shout and the spirituals of Afro-American converts to evangelical Protestantism. In addition, the slaves' rich heritage of folk belief and folk expression was not destroyed but was augmented by conversion.[34]

The egalitarian tendencies engendered by the participation of both black and white in the evangelical Protestant revivals was strongly resisted by most of the slave owners. To allay their fears many of the Southern churchmen emphasised that their plantation missions represented no threat to slavery, but rather the opposite. They advocated a Christian social order based on the Christian slave's duty to serve his master and the Christian master's duty to care for his slave. In their attempt to counter the Christian abolitionists' arguments from the North, pro-slavery apologists emphasised the positive aspects of slave evangelisation but could never completely allay the fears of some plantation owners who continued to perceive religious instruction as a threat. In the recognition of the slave's claim to humanity and his right to Christian instruction, there was indeed a subtle and implicit threat to the system of slavery. Furthermore, the suggestion that Christian slave owners had duties towards their slaves was a chink in the armour of slavery which slaves were quick to exploit and develop.[35] That some slaveholders professed to be Christian apparently did little to improve the way they treated their slaves. The brutalising continued and in some cases even increased with the 'conversion' of the slaveholder.[36]

In 1844–45, the Methodist and Baptist churches in the North split from the South over the slavery issue, with the Northern churches championing abolition while those in the South, having somewhat allayed the fears of the slaveholders, sought to justify their position by an increased effort to convert and instruct slaves. However, because of the anti-literacy laws, religious knowledge was only communicated orally.[37]

The Presbyterians, Lutherans and Episcopalians did not split along the Mason Dixon line until secession and the outbreak of the American Civil War, and then the divisions were political rather than being a moral reaction to the slavery issue.[38] H. Richard Niebuhr notes that:

One error of popular belief, however, must be guarded against in considering the character of the schism between Northern and Southern Christianity ... that the divergent judgements on slavery were due, in the main, to any excellence of disinterested moral insight on the part of the North is an untenable rationalisation of the true process by which such a social judgement comes to pass. The difference in attitude towards slavery was rooted in a difference of economic interest and structure, of culture and tradition.... The Northern condemnation of slavery was made possible by the whole economic development of the states north of the Mason and Dixon line.... The Southern defence of the institution was eventually due to the rising importance of cotton in the world's markets and to the invention of the cotton gin. Prior to the establishment of cotton as king the South had given almost as much voice to the demand for the liberation of slaves as the North.[39]

WRITINGS AND REVOLTS

As a result of missionary activity, particularly that of the Society for the Propagation of the Gospel, some slaves and ex-slaves had become literate and, not surprisingly, the petitions for the abolition of slavery, written by black people themselves from the last quarter of the sixteenth Century, employed many religious arguments and quotations from the Scriptures. In particular, the black Christian community felt a close affinity with the oppressed Israelites and with their God who, as the Lord of Hosts, delivered His people and defeated their enemies. The story of the Exodus from bondage in Egypt and the ultimate arrival at the promised land was for the slave the prototype of his own longed for deliverance.[40]

Robert Alexander Young's 'Ethiopian Manifesto' and David Walker's 'Appeal to the coloured Citizens of the World', both written in 1829, made extensive appeals to the Bible as justification for the abolition of slavery, and condemned 'the cruelties inflicted on us by the enlightened Christians of America'.[41] At the same time however, Walker recognised that some whites 'in truth and indeed ... were the people of God'.[42] Near the end of his book he pleads with the whites of America:

> Throw away your fears and prejudices.... Treat us then like men, and we will be your friends. And there is not a doubt in my mind, but that the whole of the past will be sunk into oblivion, and we yet, under God, will become a united and happy people. The whites may say it is impossible, but remember that nothing is impossible with God.[43]

The alternative to such a solution was also clearly spelt out: violent rebellion.

When slave insurrections did take place, two of the motivating factors were the use of the Scriptures and African religious beliefs. While white Christian abolitionists also used the Bible to justify the dismantling of slavery, the black understanding was generally far more radical and included, not only freedom, but also equality and interracial brotherhood.[44] W. E. B. DuBois wrote concerning the free Negro leader of the North:

> Freedom became to him a real thing and not a dream ... this desire for freedom seized the black millions still in bondage, and became their one ideal for life.... For fifty years Negro religion thus transformed itself and identified itself with the dream of Abolition, until that which was a radical fad in the white North and an anarchistic plot in the white South had become a religion to the black world.[45]

For the Southern Negro, the planning of slave insurrections was most conveniently accomplished on Sundays when white people were in church, some leisure was available and slaves could gather for a 'religious' meeting. Here the desire for freedom from sin could easily become the wish for freedom from white oppression, and because conspiracies and rebellions were often linked to religious meetings, many types of slave gathering – including public funerals and holiday feasts – were banned in parts of the Southern States and in the West Indies.[46] Wilmore notes that:

> ... even in the numerous slave revolts prior to 1800, religious factors of one sort or another are not to be discounted. Some times visionary white men, marginal to their own societies' norms and customs, were involved. At other times, African conjurers or witch doctors who had received their basic training in the Caribbean were sometimes in the background. At still other times, Black 'jack-legged' preachers – some of them undoubtedly practised in the lore of African and West Indian religions – men of extraordinary intelligence and influence over their fellows, kept the pot boiling by relating slavery with the white man's immorality, and freedom with the black man's eternal salvation.[47]

From the beginning of the nineteenth Century there is increasing evidence of black Christianity's involvement with the struggle for freedom. In 1822 the majority of the thirty-seven slaves executed for involvement in the Denmark Vesey plot were members of the African Methodist Church in Charleston. Vesey was apparently well versed in the Scriptures and used them to condemn the practice of slavery. Another leader, 'Gullah' Jack

Pritchard was both a member of the African Methodist church and an exponent of conjuration.[48]

The black minister, Nat Turner saw the God of the Bible as a demander of justice, and Christianity as liberation from all earthly bondage. For him, as for many other black preachers of the time, Christ was perceived as continuing in the same tradition as the prophets of the Old Testament: calling down the wrath of God upon the oppressors of His people and championing social justice. The 'Old Testament religion' of the blacks stood in stark contrast to that of most whites who emphasised Jesus as the Lamb of God, always obedient to His heavenly master – the suffering servant.

Turner, believing himself called of God and 'ordained for some great purpose in the hands of the Almighty', reported having received many signs and visions from the Holy Spirit before the eclipse of the sun in February 1831 and a strange atmospheric phenomenon in August convinced him that the time had come for his apocalyptic struggle with the 'Serpent' of the slavery system. By August 23rd at least seventy people were involved in the killing of between sixty and seventy-five whites. Twelve slaves were transported, twenty, including Turner, were hanged and many more were lynched. Over one hundred Negroes died in the uprising. If freedom could not be attained in life, then to die in its pursuit meant release from slavery:

> Oh freedom! Oh freedom!
> Oh! freedom, I love thee!
> And before I'll be a slave,
> I'll be buried in my grave,
> And go home to my Lord and be free.[49]

As a result of the Turner revolt, legislation was passed throughout the South prohibiting slaves from acquiring literacy and forbidding blacks to preach. DuBois states:

Virginia declared, in 1831, that neither slaves nor free Negroes might preach, nor could they attend religious service at night without permission. In North Carolina slaves and free Negroes were forbidden to preach, exhort, or teach 'in prayer meetings or other association for worship where slaves of different families are collected together' on penalty of not more than thirty-nine lashes. Maryland and Georgia had similar laws. The Mississippi law of 1831 said, It is 'unlawful for any slave, free Negro, or mulatto to preach the gospel' upon pain of receiving thirty-nine lashes upon the naked back....[50]

For the black Christian community, being able to worship God was associated with the hope of ultimate freedom from white oppression, even as Moses' demand to Pharoah that the Israelites be granted freedom to worship God in the mountain was the prelude to freedom from Egyptian bondage.

THE RISE OF INDEPENDENT BLACK CHURCHES

> In forcing blacks to become English in language, American in culture, Christian in beliefs, and repressed in social, political, economic, and ecclesiastical spheres, they were coerced into creating independent black churches, denominations, sects, and cults.[51]

As a result of anti-black prejudices and segregation in the predominantly white churches, and the Negro desire for self-determination, by the last quarter of the eighteenth century several independent black Baptist congregations and the Free African Society of Richard Allen and Absalom Jones had been formed in the North. The latter, though patterned on the class meetings of early Methodism, was primarily concerned with community action and social welfare. It was established to serve the social, political, economic and educational needs of black people and became involved in abolitionist activity. In 1790 the holding of regular religious services became part of its function but, although ethical standards were set, there was no reference to creeds and ordinances. This society created what Wilmore describes as, '... the classic pattern for the black church in the United States. A pattern of religious commitment that has a double focus – the free and autonomous worship of God in the way Black people worship him, and the unity and social welfare of the Black community'.[52]

In 1787, because of being segregated and banned from taking communion, the Negro members of two Methodist societies in Baltimore left to organise the Baltimore African Church. In Philadelphia on 17 July 1794, the St. Thomas' African

Episcopal church was dedicated with Absalom Jones as pastor, and twelve days later Bishop Francis Asbury preached the dedicatory sermon at the Mother Bethel African Methodist Episcopal Church, pastored by Richard Allen who was ordained a deacon by Asbury. In 1816, sixteen people representing these and other black churches in Delaware and Pennsylvania met in General Convention at the Bethel Church in Philadelphia to elect Daniel Coker as Bishop and to 'become one body under the name and style of the African Methodist Episcopal Church'. Coker resigned the following day to become a missionary in Africa and Allen became Bishop.[53] In 1800, a group of black Methodists in New York City had withdrawn from the predominantly white church to establish the Zion Church, and on 21 June 1821 they met with representatives from New Haven, Philadelphia and Long Island to form their own denomination: the African Methodist Episcopal Zion Church.[54]

Both of these black Methodist denominations were strongly opposed to slavery and were concerned with the physical as well as the spiritual welfare of the black community. Also both provided support for slave rebellions and stations for fugitives using the Underground Railroad. There were also black Presbyterian, Episcopal, Congregational and Methodist churches which remained within the predominantly white denominations but these were generally less militant and black-orientated than the African Methodists and the Baptists.[55]

Because of their independent congregational church policy, the Baptists in the South offered black members more opportunity for involvement in church business, although this was conducted under white supervision. The First African Church of Savannah, Georgia, was formed – in the midst of severe persecution – by the slave Andrew Bryan in 1778, and by 1815 had a congregation of 2417. By 1821 the black Gillfield Baptist Church of Petersburg, Virginia, which had been admitted to the Portsmouth Baptist Association in 1810, had grown to a membership of 441 and had the largest congregation in the association. By 1851 this had increased to 1361.

Efforts to curtail the independence of these and other black churches resulted, at least in part, from the implication of some black ministers and members in slave revolts and conspiracies. During the 1830s, some separate African Baptist Churches were forced to merge with white congregations, others were closed while a few, including the two mentioned above, not only survived in the face of intense pressure from white ecclesiastical and secular authorities but even thrived.[56] Raboteau notes that: '... by the time of emancipation there were black churches in the South with histories that extended back fifty – and in a few cases, seventy-five years'.[57] DuBois quotes a figure of 468 000 black church members in the South by 1859, and within forty years of emancipation almost one-third of the Negro population were church members.[58]

Before the Civil War, the orthodox position of churches in the South was that Negroes were sub-human and there could be neither human or spiritual brotherhood with them. The 'heretical' who challenged this were forcibly silenced. After emancipation, black Christians were expelled from the white Churches in the South and this compelled them to form their own black denominations. Such segregated worship remains the norm in the Southern States today.

The setting up of independent black churches was not motivated by a wish to re-establish elements of traditional African religion, but by a desire to exercise spiritual and ecclesiastical authority. It was a step towards black self determination and it stressed that for black people Christianity is community. In this respect black Christianity echoed the ethnic community of African folk religion. Under different circumstances blacks might have become fully integrated into the predominantly white-controlled denominations. But not only were they generally denied positions of leadership, they were also segregated, discriminated against and treated as inferior by white Christians. It was not because of a lack of theological sophistication that black Christians were rejected but simply because they were black. In the white churches of both the North and the South, belief in the dogma of the inferiority of the Negro and superiority of the white man was taken for granted, justified sometimes by fanciful interpretations of the Biblical reference to the curse of Ham, and sometimes by identifying the Negro with the serpent which tempted Eve.[59]

White disdain could not prevent many black ministers from becoming influential through their writings on slavery, theology and pan-Africanism. Perhaps the most notable and militant Black Presbyterian minister was Henry Highland Garnet who, at the National Negro Convention in 1843, delivered his Address

to the Slaves of the United States' in which he appealed to those
in bondage 'in the name of the merciful God' to plead their own
cause with the slave holders – 'tell them plainly, that you are
determined to be free' – resist their tyranny and be prepared to
'die freemen' rather 'than live to be slaves', 'Liberty', he said, 'is
a spirit sent out from God, and like its great Author, is no
respecter of persons. ...Awake, awake; millions of voices are
calling you! Your dead fathers speak to you from their graves.
Heaven, as with a voice of thunder, calls on you to arise from the
dust. Let your motto be resistance! *resistance!* RESISTANCE!'[60]

Another prominent and influential Christian in the Negro
Convention of the mid-nineteenth Century, was the physician,
journalist and lay theologian, Martin R. Delaney. Delaney was a
proponent of black American immigration to Africa and black
nationalism. He believed that black missions should carry
Christianity to their ancestral homeland. However, he was
critical of the adoption by black churches of the Protestant
evangelical view that a person's physical condition was dependent on his spiritual or moral state. If this were true, he argued,
God would not prosper white people and place black people in
bondage when whites were guilty of the greater wickedness. He
argued that it was foolish for blacks to seek equality and self
improvement by praying for it because the universe is governed
by spiritual, moral, and physical laws which operate indepen-
dently of one another. Hence, a spiritual blessing results from
prayer, a moral good from exercising one's sense of justice, and a
physical end from the use of physical means. Spiritual means
would not suffice to equip the black person to compete with
whites in the moral and physical arenas. It was a theology of
racial redemption which included a struggle against the powers
of political and social evil, an exodus from the land of their
captivity to an appointed place which he ultimately identified as
West Africa, and the evangelisation of Africa by black
Americans.[61]

Similar sentiments were expressed by the black Episcopal
clergyman, Alexander Crommell, the A. M. E. Bishop, Henry
McNeil Turner and the academic, Edward William Blyden.
Blyden, in particular, interpreted the forcible removal of
millions of Africans from their native land in terms of God's
providence: first, that they might be trained to civilise and
evangelise their homeland; second, by making them long for

escape from persecution and deprivation; third, by bringing a portion of them back to Africa and, fourth, by keeping their fatherland for them in their absence.[62] A similar understanding of God's providence is to be found among many of the Jamaican Pentecostals in Britain who perceive their migration from the Caribbean to the United Kingdom in search of work as God's means of bringing the gospel back to the people who once brought it to them. Unlike most of the black Pentecostals in Britain, however, many of the early black ministers and theologians in America were deeply involved in politics which they saw as a legitimate means of Christian action.[63] The majority of black first generation Pentecostals in Britain totally reject political action as a means of improving their lot and tend to rely on supernatural solutions. These solutions however, are not simply 'other worldly', for the power of God is perceived as with them and in them to save and to heal and to build the Church in the midst of the concrete realities of racist urban England.

The American Civil War and the emancipation of the slaves in the South resulted in the merging of the institutional black churches which were mainly in the North, with the 'invisible institution' of the church which had developed among the slaves of the South. Although the integration of the two streams of black Christianity was achieved, it was not without some internal divisions. The Negroes who had been free before the Civil War, many of whom were educated mulattos, despised what they considered to be the primitive nature of worship among the recently emancipated masses.[64]

By the end of the nineteenth century, the independent black churches in America had established extensive links with black churches in Africa, many of which became involved with the struggle for independence from colonial rule which were to continue throughout the first half of the twentieth century.[65]

THE EMBOURGEOISEMENT OF THE BLACK CHURCHES

While the influence of black Christianity in Africa was promoting radicalism and nationalism, the black churches in America were increasingly conforming to white conservative evangelicalism. From the turn of the century many Negroes, especially light-skinned mulattos who had been educated, were, in spite of discrimination, moving into the lower-middle class, and it was in this stratum that most of the church members were located. The poor Negroes of the South, many of whom were later to move to the urban ghettos seeking a better way of life, often found that they were treated with disdain by their fellows who had risen in the socio-economic scale. Wilmore writes that:

> School teachers, college educators, government employees and most of the northern based bishops of the three major Methodist bodies were generally members of this relatively privileged class which in some respects rivalled the white middle class in culture, exclusiveness and sophistication. ... By the end of the First World War, the independent Black churches in the United States were becoming respectable institutions. Having rejected the Black nationalism of Turner they turned more and more towards white Christianity to find a prototype of authentic spirituality.[66]

At the start of the twentieth century, the black Christian militancy and nationalism of slave folk tradition, which had been exemplified by Bishop Henry M. Turner, was being overtaken by the philosophy of self-improvement and gradualism advocated by Booker T. Washington. This philosophy conformed to the ethics of white conservative evangelicalism which particularly focused on the ideal of the non-violent, patiently suffering white Christ.[67] Such was the situation among the black churches on the eve of the birth of the Pentecostal movement under the inspired leadership of the black Holiness preacher, Bishop William Joseph Seymour.

There was always tension between the dominant European understanding of Christianity and that which developed as an Afro-Christian synthesis in response to the conditions of slavery. Black proletarian religion was simultaneously both less than and more than European Christianity. It rejected much of what was irrelevant to the needs of black people and it re-affirmed many of the folk beliefs of West Africa.

AFRICAN RETENTIONS IN BLACK CHRISTIANITY

Wilmore summarises the underlying African elements in the black religious community of the United States, as consisting of:

> ... A deep sense of the pervasive reality of the spirit world, the blotting out of the line between the sacred and the profane, the practical use of religion in all of life; reverence for ancestors and their real or symbolic presence with us, the corporateness of social life, the source of evil in the consequences of an act rather than in the act itself, and the imaginative and creative use of rhythm – singing and dancing – in the celebration of life and the worship of God. All of these aspects of African religions were found in some form, however attenuated, in the black religion of the 18th and 19th centuries and were absorbed into black christianity in the Caribbean, South America and the United States.[68]

More specifically, Herskovits suggests that 'spirit possession by the Holy Ghost' which inspired 'motor behaviour that is not European but African', rhythmic hand clapping, the antiphonal participation of the congregation in the sermon, the immediacy of God in the services and baptism by immersion, are all survivals of Africanisms.[69] However, because of the similarity of some religious traits of both African and European origin, it is very difficult, if not impossible in some instances, to determine which of them are survivals of African religious practices, which were adopted by Negro slaves because of their similarity to African religious traditions and which of them appealed to the slave community for reasons unconnected with African religion.[70] What is certain is that a holistic world view, the ethnic worshipping community, spirit possession, spirit healing, spirit power, dreams, trances, antiphonal responses, music, rhythm, dancing and other motor behaviour all have African antecedents. During the frontier camp meetings of the late eighteenth and early nineteenth centuries, and the revivalist and Pentecostal services of the twentieth century, black participants were generally noisier, more active and displayed greater spontaneity, rhythm, dance and enthusiastic motor behaviour than their white counterparts.[71]

Raboteau, writing of the eighteenth and nineteenth century camp-meetings, maintains that the physical manifestations among black people were not primarily the outlet for an oppressed people to release their frustrations and tensions, nor were they due to any innate emotionalism, but rather, ... the slaves tended to express religious emotion in certain patterned types of bodily movement influenced by the African heritage of dance'.[72] The camp-meeting revivals, continues Raboteau,

> ... where enthusiastic and ecstatic religious behaviour was encouraged, presented a congenial setting for slaves to merge African patterns of response with Christian interpretations of the experience of spirit possesson, an experience shared by both black and whites. ... While the American slaves danced under the impulses of the Spirit of a 'new' god, they danced in ways their fathers in Africa would have recognised.[73]

Such behaviour was not limited to the camp-meetings, but became the norm in many black churches. Wherever it appeared it was severely criticised by many of the white clergy and those black ministers who were members of the rising acculturated Negro middle class.[74]

In the mid-nineteenth century, Frederick Law Olmsted described his visit to a black church in New Orleans where he witnessed the following behaviour in response to the preaching: trembling, chattering teeth, convulsions of the face, antiphonal responses such as shouts, groans, and shreaks, stamping, jumping, clapping and dancing.[75] While such manifestations were not restricted to black religionists, they were generally more common among them and more extreme. Furthermore, although the pneumatology differs between the spirit possession of African primal folk religion and the Spirit baptism or 'getting the Spirit' of black Christianity, the music and motor behaviour associated with it display considerable evidence of continuity. Shouting, antiphonal responses, repetitious singing, glossolalia, clapping, foot tapping, stamping, jumping, swaying the body, alternately shifting the weight from one foot to the other, dancing and other motor behaviour, were all practised in West African religion and slave Christianity, and continue to be common among black Pentecostals in the United States, Jamaica and Britain today.[76] It may be argued that white revivalists and Pentecostals displayed the same religious behaviour – though usually in an attenuated form – and that this contradicts the view that these practises are of African origin.

However, there is evidence which suggests that black patterns of religious behaviour influenced the whites who attended the same camp-meetings in the 18th and 19th centuries and those who were involved with the birth and development of the Pentecostal movement at the beginning of the 20th century. In fact, the degree of enthusiasm demonstrated at religious meetings was often proportionate to the number of black people in the congregation![77] Herskovits writes that: '...the tradition of violent possession associated with the earliest camp-meetings is far more African than European, and hence there is reason to hold that, in part at least, it was inspired in the whites by their contact with Negroes'.[78]

Just as African music was the basis for the music of the slaves, and this in turn gave rise to the blues, jazz, rock-and-roll and much of contemporary popular and 'gospel' music, so also the influence of African religious ecstaticism and spirit possession is evident not only among black Pentecostals but also in an attenuated form among the white Pentecostals in the United States and, to a lesser extent, in Britain.[79]

BLACK CHRISTIAN MUSIC

The music of black slaves was strongly influenced by their African heritage, and defied the best efforts of Europeans to reduce it to conventional musical notation.[80] It was characterised by 'a strong emphasis on call and response, polyrhythms, syncopation, ornamentation, slides from one note to another, and repetition'.[81] The words expressed Biblical themes and the music was influenced by Western hymnody and secular music, but the style of the 'Negro Spiritual' was African.[82]

The Spiritual was an expression of the oral theology and emotional fervour of the Christian slave community, a powerful means of communicating the gospel by preaching through song and of uniting the worshippers in the celebration of life. The black understanding of the Bible was translated into song and made relevant to the daily experience of the slave. It was a means of transmitting religious ideas, of expressing the depth of sorrow and suffering they were forced to endure, and of declaring – albeit covertly – their resistance to slavery and their longing for freedom.[83]

One ex-slave from Kentucky claimed that Spirituals were created by using African tunes and Biblical themes.

Us ole heads use ter make 'em on de spurn of de moment, after we wrestle wid de Spirit and come thoo. But the tunes was brung from Africa by our grandaddies. Dey was jis 'miliar songs' ... dey calls 'em Spirituals, case de Holy Spirit done revealed 'em to 'em. Some say Moss Jesus taught 'em, and 'I's seed 'em start in meetin'. We'd all be at the 'prayer house' de Lord's Day, and de White preacher he'd splain de word and read whar Ezekiel done say: Dry bones gwine ter lib again. And, honey, de Lord would come a-shining thoo dem pages and revive dis ole nigger's heart, and I'd jump up dar and den and holler and shout and sing and pat, and dey would all cotch de words ... and dey's all take it up and keep at it, and keep a addin' to it and den it would be a spiritual.[84]

The Spirituals were improvised and extemporised to the rhythms of stamping feet, clapping hands and swaying bodies, and they served, not only spiritual, but also social functions. They were a means of reinforcing group identity and social solidarity, particularly in times of crisis and suffering such as funerals and beatings at the hands of slave holders. They also speak of hope, faith in the ultimate justice of God, and of joy.

The symbolic or allegorical nature of the Spirituals ensured an ambiguity whereby their meaning and significance among the slave community could be altered to meet challenging individual and group needs for solace, comfort and hope for the future. They were also a means of expressing their protests and anger against the inhumanity of their bondage. They were not, as some have presumed, merely concerned with other-worldly goals, but expressed the demands of slaves for social and political freedom, and were an affirmation of black dignity and personhood. Negro Spirituals were simultaneously theological, political, social, cultural and historical.[85] Thus the Spirituals communicated at two or more levels: the spiritual and the political, the sacred and the profane. However, we must remember that West African primal religions do not make the distinction between sacred and secular, and slaves continued to perceive the spirit world as interacting with the material world.[86]

Terms such as 'Canaan', 'de promised land', 'de oder side of Jordan', 'heaven' and 'home' in Negro Spirituals were as much references to the lands of freedom – the northern United States, Canada and Africa – as they were to the Biblical heaven. Furthermore, if Cone is correct, such references were also an affirmation of personhood, a kind of inaugurated eschatology which brought the future into the present.[87] If black people were to live in heaven in the future it was because they were God's children now, and they were on their way to heaven now in spite of the cruelty and servitude which was their daily experience. Cone writes:

> Blacks were able, through song, to transcend the enslavement of the present and to live as if the future had already come. Hope, in the black spirituals ... believes that the historical is in motion, moving towards a divine fulfilment. It is the belief that things can be radically otherwise than they are: that reality is not fixed, but is moving in the direction of human liberation.[88]

Thus slaves were able, not only to look beyond the cruel realities of their present bondage but also to change the present to conform to a future which was not only freedom in heaven for the dead but also the apocalyptic end of history inaugurated by the Second Advent of Christ. Then God would right every wrong, judge the oppressor and free the oppressed.[89]

The Spirituals which speak of liberation deal with more than freedom from sin. They declare that the God who delivered Israel from Egyptian slavery will deliver black people from their bondage:

> Oh Mary, don't you weep, don't you moan,
> Oh Mary, don't you weep, don't you moan,
> Pharoah's army got drownded,
> Oh Mary don't you weep.
>
> When Israel was in Egypt's land,
> Let my people go;
> Oppressed so hard they could not stand,
> Let my people go;
> Go down Moses, way down in Egypt's land;
> Tell ole Pharoah
> Let my people go.[90]

With the decision of Abraham Lincoln to wage war on the South and proclaim the emancipation of the slaves – which was perceived by many blacks as God working in history on their behalf in the same way as in Israel's Exodus – the ambiguity of their songs disappeared:

> Slavery chain done broke at last,
> broke at last, broke at last,
> Slavery chain done broke at last,
> Goin to praise God till I die.
>
> Freedom at last!
> Freedom at last!
> Great God-a-mighty,
> Freedom at last![91]

SEYMOUR'S HERITAGE

By the beginning of the twentieth century the black churches of the United States had become to a large extent conformed to white middle-class conservative evangelicalism, and many Negroes and mulattos had moved up the social scale.[92] Both black and white working class fundamentalists were dissatisfied with the 'deadness' in the churches and there was a general agreement among the Holiness people that the Second Advent was imminent and would be preceded by a revival of worldwide magnitude.

Black people, particularly those whose lot had not been improved by upward social mobility, were also concerned that freedom had not brought about acceptance either outside or inside the churches. Black Christian abolitionists had cried out for more than freedom. They had proclaimed that God demanded equality for black people. The twentieth-century Pentecostal movement was born at a time when fundamentalist Christians were anticipating the Second Advent and blacks were seeking a solution to the inequalities in American society. For many, the Pentecostal movement appeared to promise the impending fulfilment of both dreams.

If Pentecostalism has a founder, then it was the black Holiness preacher, William Joseph Seymour. Born in the Southern States in 1870, entered the world just five years after the abolition of slavery, and grew up in the midst of bitter and violent colour prejudice. The black man was free but he was not equal. Racism was institutionalised in policies which denied black people the vote, segregated them from whites and ensured their continued subjugation.

Summarising Seymour's first twenty-four years of life, Douglas J. Nelson writes:

> Seymour receives little of no formal schooling but works hard, educates himself ... drinks in the 'invisible institution' of black folk Christianity, learns to love the great Negro spirituals, has visions of God, and becomes an earnest student of unfulfilled scriptural prophecy.[93]

Pre-eminent in his socialisation was the Bible and, as Nelson states, 'the "invisible institution" of black folk Christianity' with its themes of freedom, equality and community. Freedom from slavery, oppression and injustice as well as freedom from sin and freedom to let ones being – mind, body and emotions – become totally involved in the power and presence of the Spirit of God. Equality among men for 'God is no respecter of persons.'[94] The recognition of black personhood and black dignity. Black men and women made in the image of God and in this world – here and now – the children of God. The congregation as the community of God's people. Not merely individuals standing alone in a vertical relationship to God, but the family of God in horizontal relationship with each other. The relevance of religion in all of life, the nearness of the spirit world and the interaction between and the integration of the sacred and the profane. The revolutionary desire for and expectation of the cataclysmic Second Advent of the Lord Jesus Christ to exalt the poor, the humble and the downtrodden, put down the high, the mighty and the oppressor and right every wrong. The desire and search for the spiritual power of God to accomplish in the world what man – particularly the black man with his limited social and political outlets – could not achieve by his own endeavour. A religion that was primarily oral in its liturgy and theology: that was expressed in the story, the shout, the song, the dance and other distinctively African motor behaviour, to the accompanyment of the polyrhythmic clapping of hands stamping of feet and swaying of bodies. A spirituality which transcended that of white middle-class Christianity; which opened the black person up to the divine in a personal way which affected his or her daily living.

Seymour grew up as a black Christian, not merely because he was a Christian with a black skin but because he inherited the religion of this community which was that particular form of Christianity which had developed as a synthesis of African and European belief systems during slavery.

Those recurring sentiments, themes, principles, aims, ideas and ideals which are to be found in African folk religion became the leitmotive of black American Christianity, and to them were added other leitmotive which were generated in the bi-cultural crucible of slavery. To West African concepts of community, spiritual power, spirit possession and the integration of the natural and supernatural, were added freedom, equality, black personhood and dignity, and the desire for revolution – the Second Advent, divine intervention or at least divine aid. The great black symphony survived the middle passage preserved in oral tradition, beaten out and danced in the polyrhythmic musical style and choreography of Africa.

Bishop Seymour and other black Americans who gathered together in Los Angeles shared a common religious heritage which was to become part of the early Pentecostal.movement and which endures in a more or less attenuated form among black Pentecostals in the United States, the Caribbean and Britain today.

3 The Roots of Pentecostalism: the American Holiness Movement

The roots of Pentecostalism lie not only in the black American understanding and practice of Christianity but also in the American Holiness Movement which grew out of Wesleyan Methodism. Frederick Dale Bruner states that, 'Methodism is the most important of the modern traditions for the student of Pentecostal origins to understand' for, as he goes on to say, 'eighteenth century Methodism is the mother of the nineteenth century American holiness movement which, in turn, bore twentieth-century Pentecostalism'.[1] It is to Wesleyan Methodism that Pentecostals owe a great deal of their theology and practice.

The Holiness Movement in the United States passed on its emotional fervour, revivalism, biblical fundamentalism, Armenian theology, teaching on divine healing, ethical rigour, rejection of ecclesiasticism and belief in the 'Second Blessing' of 'entire sanctification' to the Pentecostal movement.[2] This latter doctrine was part of one of the central tenets of John Wesley who, having imbibed the spirituality of several Catholic devotional writers and developed their idea of a post-conversion crisis, taught a post-justification experience whereby the believer is cleansed 'from all filthiness both of flesh and spirit' by a second work of grace.[3] A crude version of Methodism's 'entire sanctification' or 'holiness' teaching influenced the Great Awakening in America during the eighteenth century and became the handmaid of revivalism. During the 1830s Charles Grandison Finney redefined entire sanctification as a willingness to become involved in social action as an outworking of personal faith and consecration. This became known as Oberlin perfectionism – named after Oberlin College of which Finney became President.[4]

Throughout the 1830s, 1840s and 1850s, Methodism reaffirmed its belief in the doctrine of entire sanctification as the Holiness Movement challenged it to return to its roots. Holiness people also propagated the doctrine among other Protestant denominations. The spread of sanctification beliefs often strengthened the anti-slavery lobby as many Holiness people saw that Christianity and slavery were antithetical. In 1844 Methodism split between North and South over this issue.[5]

During the 1857–58 revival, holiness in either its Wesleyan or Oberlin forms was embraced by most major Protestant denominations.[6] This awakening, however, was almost entirely limited to the urban Northern states with the South virtually untouched by either the revival or the holiness doctrine. As Synan declares: 'From about 1830 until the outbreak of war, Southern theological energies were directed toward supporting and defending the institution of slavery.'[7]

The industrial expansion which followed the American Civil War was accompanied by widespread materialism and social dislocation. The churches responded with a call to holiness which resulted in nationwide prayer meetings, conventions, camp meetings and the establishment of a variety of Holiness associations.

THE EMBOURGEOISEMENT OF AMERICAN PROTESTANTISM

During the second half of the nineteenth century the Evangelical Protestant churches in the northern and western United States prospered within the new socio-economic climate created by urban industrialisation. This growth in membership and increased prosperity was accompanied by the embourgeoisement of the working-class converts who had been reached by a century of revivalism. The adoption of the protestant ethic and the arrival of immigrants who entered the social structure at the bottom, combined to create upward social mobility.[8] The now predominantly middle-class churches began to adopt the values of the secular culture. Conversion, personal piety and social service were replaced by education, prestige and materialism. Evangelism was directed towards the middle class and away from frontier regions and the urban working class. Church buildings became more ornate and were built in more fashion-able residential districts. Worship became increasingly formal and professional singers and organists were hired. Anderson writes that:

> In the last quarter of the 19th century, the identification of Protestantism with middle class culture was almost comple-te.... The Gospel of Wealth, a conglomeration of the doctrines of individualism, classical economics and social Darwinism, if not advocated by all clergymen, was proclaimed by a sufficient number to give it the apparent endorsement of Protestantism as a whole.[9]

THE HOLINESS REJECTION OF 'WORLDLINESS'

There were however dissenting voices. The predominantly working-class Holiness people, both black and white, deplored the churches' adoption of middle-class culture and secularism, but shared its social conservatism while concentrating on individual moral character as the source and solution of both personal and social problems. They condemned liberal theolo-gy, higher criticism, and biological and social evolutionary theories which they saw as undermining the miraculous and the authority of the Scriptures.[10]

In the 1880s the Social Gospel movement arose within the church to challenge the status quo and campaign for social reform on behalf of the disadvantaged. However, the Holiness people saw this as a denial of personal experiential Christianity.[11]

Thus the largely working-class Holiness minority – particu-larly in the rural South and Mid-West – drew away from the 'worldliness' of the predominantly middle class majority, while they in turn, recoiled at the 'fanatical and puritanical' attitudes of the Holiness people. With the realisation that reformation and purification within the churches was unlikely, Holiness evangelists in rural areas began to urge the faithful to leave the 'worldly', 'cold', 'formal', churches and to conform to strict standards of holiness, both internal and external. Holiness associations and organisations came into being and were condemned by the Methodist bishops as separatist. The doctrine of sanctification as a second work of grace came under attack, and by the mid-1890s Methodism had largely rejected it. At the same time, some Holiness preachers and evangelists – many of whom were later to become leaders in the Pentecostal movement – reported and indeed encouraged extraordinary 'manifestations of the Spirit' including miracles, healings, visions and glossolalia. [12]

External standards of 'holiness': taboos, and prohibitions concerning food, clothing, jewellery, cosmetics, 'worldly amusements' and the use of medicines or doctors accompanied other teachings and practises – 'sinless perfection', 'marital purity', and a third work of grace – which even some Holiness people opposed as extremist. [13]

During the last decade of the nineteenth century 'the third blessing heresy', as some dubbed it, had become influential. Originating with Benjamin Hardin Irwin – who taught that a 'baptism with the Holy Ghost and fire' should follow the second blessing of sanctification – the third blessing teaching was accompanied by outbursts of emotional fervour such as shouting, screaming, glosslalia, trances and the 'jerks'. While Irwin's Fire Baptised movement did not teach that glossolalia was the initial evidence of a person having received the Spirit baptism, there were manifestations of it, and the 'third blessing' doctrine brought one section of the Holiness movement into acceptance of an experience of power subsequent to sanctification. Such a teaching was later to be adopted by the Pentecostal movement. Although rejected by the majority of Holiness people, Irwin's teaching gained many adherents, particularly in the rural Mid-West and the South. [14]

By the beginning of the twentieth century the zeal or fanaticism of the Holiness movement had largely burnt itself out and many of its supporters had left. The remnant increased the degree of organisation and regulation in an attempt to correct the deficiency in the church structure which they believed was responsible for the decline. This gave rise to the Church of the Nazarene and other groups which were later to merge with it. Revivalist evangelists placed restraints upon extreme emotionalism, and ecstatic experiences which, if they were to occur at all, were now confined to the pulpit. [15] Revivalistic campaigns lost their spontaneity, 'quenched the Spirit' and became highly organised business ventures which relied on techniques to get results. The restraints imposed by the Holiness denominations and revivalists resulted in many dissatisfied Holiness people leaving to form new groups.[16]

By the beginning of the twentieth century there had also been a change in the terminology used by the Holiness people to express their belief in the second blessing. Increasingly the experience was referred to as the 'Baptism of the Holy Ghost'.[17] Associated with this terminological shift was a change from Christocentrism to an increasing emphasis on the Holy Spirit, and an exegetical shift from the Old Testament, the Gospels and Epistles to the Acts of the Apostles and the prophecy in Joel, Chapter 2 accompanied by a growing eschatological emphasis. The power and gifts of the Spirit – particularly healing – also received increasing attention, and pneumatic experiences were sought by many as evidence of having received the second blessing.[18]

THE KESWICK MOVEMENT

During the last quarter of the nineteenth century, the Keswick Movement in Britain under the influence of the dispensational teaching of John Nelson Darby, rejected the Wesleyan view that sanctification and baptism in the Holy Spirit are synonymous. The influence of the Anglicans and Calvinists, who dominated the movement, led to sanctification being understood as an ongoing process which begins at conversion but is never completed in this life. Baptism in the Holy spirit was viewed as a separate 'enduement of power'. Leading American revivalists adopted the Keswick view of Spirit baptism and many Holiness people looked forward in anticipation to a Pentecostal revival. References to gifts of healing appear in the literature of this period, as do occasional references to glossolalia. However, glossolalia was not understood as a necessary evidence of Spirit baptism.[19]

By the end of the nineteenth century the Holiness camp was split into three main factions: those who understood sanctification and baptism in the Holy Spirit to be the same act of grace, primarily concerned with removing indwelling sin; those who believed that sanctification was a second act of grace and Spirit baptism a third; and the Keswick movement which held to the view that sanctification was a gradual ongoing process and baptism in the Spirit an enduement of power.[20] 'Yet, by the turn of the century,' writes Anderson, 'nearly all Holiness people were agreed on the imminent, premillenial, apocalyptic Second Coming of Christ, preceded by a great world-wide revival of Pentecostal dimensions.'[21]

Isolated revivals did break out at the beginning of the twentieth century, the most notable of which were in Australia under Ruben A. Torrey and in Wales under Evan Roberts. The latter was marked by a spontaneity and spiritual liberty which were later to be hallmarks of the early Pentecostal movement.[22]

4 Charles F. Parham and the Evidence Doctrine

The Holy Spirit ... reserves the speaking on other tongues as the evidence of His own incoming ... modern leaders and Holy Ghost teachers all have their private evidence of their so-called gift of the Holy Ghost; while they have failed to seek, obtain and honor the only Bible sign given as the evidence of the baptism of the Holy Ghost.

Charles Fox Parham

One by one everyone who received the Holy Spirit began to speak in other tongues as the Spirit gave them utterance. I felt satisfied that God was giving His own evidence to every one of us.

Agnes N. Osman

The individual primarily responsible for the teaching that glossolalia is the evidence of a person having received the baptism in the Holy Spirit was Charles Fox Parham. Born in Iowa in 1873, Parham believed himself to have been called 'to the ministry ... when about nine years of age'. As yet unconverted, he began to read the Bible and while rounding up cattle preached sermons to them 'on the realities of a future life'. Converted at thirteen years of age, Parham at sixteen attended a Methodist College to prepare for the ministry but soon changed his mind and began studying medicine. However, after a serious illness – during the course of which he took large quantities of morphine – it was 'revealed' to him that education was a hindrance in the service of God. He abandoned his studies and at the age of eighteen was licensed by a Methodist denomination. During the first year of an almost fruitless pastorate he came under the influence of a Quaker – his wife's grandfather – who persuaded him to abandon the doctrine of eternal torment in favour of total annihilation. Parham also rejected water baptism, accepted sanctification as a second act of grace and regarded church membership and denominational affiliation as matters of indifference. His unorthodox teachings brought him in to conflict with the Methodists and he left them in 1894.[1]

Parham came in contact with the followers of Irwin and, while rejecting the emotionalism of the Fire-Baptized movement, he adopted their view that a third experience of a 'baptism with the Holy Ghost and fire' should follow sanctification.[2]

He became a travelling evangelist, rejected all medications and laid special emphasis on divine healing. His wife, whom he married on New Year's eve, 1896, subsequently described his teaching as: '... Salvation, Healing, Sanctification, the Second Coming of Christ, and the Baptism of the Holy Spirit, although we had not then received the evidence of speaking in other tongues ...'[3]

Parham became increasingly concerned to find a teaching and experience of baptism in the Holy Spirit which he believed 'tallied with the Word of God'. In his search, he visited many Holiness Bible schools and homes, including the communtarian 'Zion City' of the megalomaniac John Alexander Dowie and the Bible and Missionary Training School of A. B. Simpson. 'I returned,' wrote Parham, 'fully convinced that while many had obtained real experience in sanctification and the anointing that abideth, there still remained a great outpouring of power for the Christians who were to close this age.'[4]

STONE'S FOLLY

Returning to his base in Topeka, Kansas, Parham obtained the use of an unfinished mansion known as 'Stone's Folly'. There, on 15 October 1900 he opened the 'College of Bethel' with some thirty-six people. Though from different denominational backgrounds, they all shared Parham's desire for a new experience of the Holy Spirit. Their 'only text-book was the Bible' and their understanding of it ultra-literal.[5]

R. M. Anderson speculates, on the basis of the available evidence, that Parham's understanding of the baptism in the Holy Spirit accompanied by glossolalia dated from sometime during 1900. Parham had long believed that God could miraculously bestow the ability to speak in foreign languages upon missionaries. He later wrote:

I had felt for years that any missionary going to the foreign field should preach in the language of the natives. That if God had ever equipped His ministers in that way he could do it today ... that anybody today ought to be able to preach in any language of the world if they had horse sense enough to let God use their tongue and throat ... I believed our experience should tally exactly with the Bible ...[6]

Near the end of December 1900, Parham left Bethel College for a three day campaign in Kansas City. Before leaving, he had instructed his students to carefully read and study the second chapter of the book of Acts which records the outpouring of the Holy Spirit on the day of Pentecost. He said to his students:

The gifts are in the Holy Spirit and with the baptism of the Holy Spirit the gifts, as well as the graces, should be manifested. Now, students, while I am gone, see if there is not some evidence given of the baptism so there may be no doubt on the subject.[7]

Upon his return to Stone's Folly on the morning of 30 December, the unanimous opinion of the students was that 'the indisputable proof' of 'the Pentecostal blessing' was that the recipients 'spake with other tongues'. The group at Bethel plus some seventy-five who had joined them for the New Year holidays committed themselves to prayer, fasting and the worship of God as they 'awaited the coming of the Spirit in a second Pentecost'.[8] Around 7 o'clock on the first day of January 1901, records Agnes Osman, '... it came into my heart to ask Bro. Parham to lay hands upon me that I might receive the gift of the Holy Spirit'.[9] As Parham prayed and laid his hands on her head she 'began to speak in tongues, glorifying God'. Parham claimed: 'I had scarcely repeated three dozen sentences when a glory fell upon her, a halo seemed to surround her head and face, and she began speaking in the Chinese language and was unable to speak English for three days.'[10]

On the evening of the 3 January, while Parham was holding a meeting elsewhere, many others at Bethel College received the same glossolalic experience. Lilian Thistlethwaite, Parham's sister-in-law, described it thus:

We prayed for ourselves, we prayed for one another. I never felt so little and utterly nothing before. A scrap of paper charred by a fire is the best description I can give of my feelings. Then through the Spirit this message came to my soul, 'Praise Him for the baptism for He does come in by faith through the laying on of hands.' Then a great joy came into my soul and I began to say, 'I praise Thee', and my tongue began to get thick and great floods of laughter came into my heart. I could no longer think words of praise, for my mind was sealed, but my mouth was filled with a rush of words I didn't understand. I tried not to laugh for I feared to grieve the Spirit. I tried to praise Him in English but could not, so I just let the praise come as it would in the new language given, with floodgates of glory wide open. He had come to me, even to me to speak not of himself but to magnify the Christ, – and oh, what a wonderful, wonderful Christ was revealed. Then I realised I was not alone for all spoke in tongues and magnified God.[11]

Another of those present claimed to have seen cloven tongues of fire, and Parham, returning from his meeting, reported seeing 'a sheen of white light' and hearing 'all the students ... talking in unknown tongues, no two talking the same language, and no one understanding his or her neighbour's speech'. He sought the experience himself: 'Right then their came a slight twist in my throat, a glory fell over me and I began to worship God in the Sweedish (sic) tongue, which later changed to other languages and continued till morning.'[12]

Parham appears to have believed in glossolalia as the evidence of Spirit baptism prior to the experience being received by the group at Bethel college. However, Agnes Osman claimed that she knew nothing of this until after her experience on 1 January 1901, and that she was the one to whom God revealed glossolalia as evidence of having received the Holy Spirit.[13]

After some interest created by newspaper coverage of the event, followed by unsuccessful attempts to spread the message, Parham and a few of his followers moved to Kansas City where he opened another Bible school. In four months the school was closed and Parham was deserted by all but his wife and sister-in-law. Even Agnes Osman left and repudiated her experience at Bethel.[14]

In the Autumn of 1903, after Parham had returned to his original emphasis on divine healing, he had a successful revival in the frontier mining town of Galena in Kansas. Healings attracted a great deal of attention and many were converted, baptised in the river and were 'enabled to speak in foreign tongues'. One newspaper reported that in three months Parham 'has healed over a thousand people and converted over 800'.[15]

Subsequent revivals led by Parham and his followers were also successful and resulted in the establishment of several 'Apostolic Faith' missions and house-meetings throughout the Tri-State District of Kansas, Missouri and Oklahoma. Moving to Texas in 1905, Parham was again successful and an independent Holiness mission became the headquarters of the Apostolic Faith movement in Texas. In December, two large houses were rented in Houston and a Bible school opened. Although run on similar lines to Bethel, it now included direct teaching by the Holy Spirit through prophecy, messages in tongues and interpretation. To this school came the black Holiness preacher William Joseph Seymour.[16]

5 The Birth of a Movement: William J. Seymour and the Azusa Mission

The work began among the colored people. God baptized several sanctified wash women with the Holy Ghost, who have been much used of Him.

William J. Seymour

The origins of the Pentecostal movement go back to a revival among the Negroes of North America at the beginning of the present century.

Walter J. Hollenweger

Pentecostalism, both Black and white, was essentially Black in origin ... the Pentecostal revival had begun in an all-Black home in an all-Black neighbourhood, under Seymour's sole guidance.

James S. Tinney

WILLIAM J. SEYMOUR

William Joseph Seymour was born in the Southern United States at Centreville, Louisiana in 1870. He grew up in the midst of Ku Klux Klan and White League lynchings and violence, and institutionalised racism and segregation. Seymour taught himself to read and imbibed the religion, culture and music of the black community.[1] Foremost in his schooling was the Bible and the distinctively black understanding of Christianity: freedom, equality, community, the experience of power from the Spirit of God, visions, and the apocalyptic Second Advent of the Lord Jesus Christ.

At twenty-five Seymour moved north to Indianapolis, Indiana where, because all but menial and unskilled occupations were closed to blacks, he worked as a waiter. In Indianapolis he joined a black congregation of the predominantly white Methodist Episcopal Church. It is probably significant that he joined a black congregation which was part of an interracial organisation, rather than the exclusively Negro Bethel African Methodist Episcopal Church which had been founded by Richard Allen. That Seymour's reason for attending Simpson Chapel Methodist Episcopal Church rather than the Bethel African Methodist Episcopal Church was more than merely geographical convenience is evidenced by the fact that Bethel was nearer to where he lived than Simpson Chapel. Nelson writes:

> Seymour's choice of the more interracial Methodist Episcopal Church was the first clear indication he gave of seeking interracial reconciliation. An earlier hint was his unusual leaving of the repressive rural Louisiana environment – not for a large Southern city – but for the traditional centre of the antebellum Underground Railroad where fugitive blacks had been welcomed and assisted to freedom. Seymour did not join any local church at Centreville where no interracial opportunities existed. It is probably not a coincidence that he departed Louisiana just as racial color lines were being imposed with increasing severity, reflecting his search for a more meaningful relationship with all other people. His choice of work in Indianapolis points to the same conclusion, for in a large downtown hotel restaurant he met whites in a surrounding where people spoke to one another.[2]

As the Methodist Episcopal Church, and Methodism in general, became more formal and middle class, its concern for racial justice and equality lessened, as did its enthusiasm for holiness. Many of the black and white working class left what they perceived to be the 'worldly' churches for the Holiness movement.[3] Seymour was one of them.

In 1900 he moved to another centre of the Underground Railroad, Cincinnati, Ohio. There Seymour came under the influence of the white integrationist evangelist Martin Wells Knapp who left both the Methodist Episcopal church and the mainline Holiness Association. His fervent preaching on the apocalyptic Second Advent of Christ and on divine healing separated him from many other Holiness people but attracted Seymour who shared these beliefs.[4]

Seymour joined the interracial Evening Light Saints; so called because they believed that a final great spiritual outpouring would be sent by God just before the end of world history. They also emphasised holiness, divine healing, racial equality and the need for Christians to reject the denominations in favour of the one true Church. And if there was to be only one true church, then it must encompass all races and colours.

The Saints in common with other sections of the Holiness movement, believed in a second work of grace whereby a person became sanctified by receiving an experience of the Holy Spirit likened to that which occurred on the day of Pentecost. Wesley had taught that sanctification had both individual and social dimensions but most white Holiness people stressed the former at the expense of the latter. For black Christians, on the other hand, the experience of the Spirit was more than personal holiness, it was also power from God to triumph over injustice and oppression in the social sphere.[5] The Saints were one of the notable exceptions to the norm which was the strict segregation of individuals and congregations by the colour line. Benjamin Quarles writes that: 'By 1900 Christianity had divided along the color line even more markedly than ever before ... the southern churches were almost completely separated.'[6]

Racism, though less violent, was also rife in the North. Although the period immediately following emancipation had been characterised by legislation designed to remove racial discrimination, the turn of the century saw a hardening of racial attitudes in the white community both inside and outside the churches. The doctrine of white superiority and supremacy was propounded by many white church leaders, scientists and the press.[7]

After contracting smallpox which left him scarred and blind in his left eye, Seymour ceased to resist the divine call and was ordained by the Saints. In 1903 he returned to the South to evangelise and search for relatives lost during slavery. Finding them in Houston, Texas, he settled there until the winter of the following year when he moved to Jackson, Missippi. The summer of 1905 saw Seymour in the pastorate of the Holiness church of the black minister Mrs Lucy Farrow. Farrow was temporarily away in Kansas as governess to the family of Charles Fox Parham. When she returned in October of the same year, she recounted to Seymour how she had experienced glossolalia in the Parham home. In order to learn more about glossolalia, Seymour enrolled in December at Parham's Bible school in Houston, Texas.[8]

Nelson describes the segregation which Seymour endured:

> ... attending classes at 9.00 each morning ... he is segregated outside the classroom beside the door carefully left ajar by Parham. In the afternoon missionary work, Seymour and Parham preach together one or more times in the black district of town. At the public evening service Seymour and other blacks sit in the rear and are not allowed to go to the altar for ministration because Parham practises strict segregation.[9]

Parham taught that glossolalia was both the evidence of a person having received the 'third experience' of the baptism of the Holy Spirit, a sign of the nearness of the end of human history and God's means of evangelising the heathen in foreign lands by preaching in their native languages. Seymour accepted this teaching but did not himself receive glossolalia at this time.[10]

At the invitation of a small black Holiness congregation, Seymour left Houston and travelled to Los Angeles to be their pastor. Unlike most of the United States at this time, there was relatively little racial segregation in the 'City of the Angels'. Furthermore, there was an atmosphere of spiritual expectancy there. The 1904–6 Welsh Revival under the leadership of Evan Roberts had inspired many. Evangelism, divine healing and the sanctification teaching of the Holiness people were widespread, and the city had at this time in excess of one hundred Holiness churches.

Between 1900 and 1910 about five and a half thousand Negroes moved into the city along with large numbers of Mexicans and Japanese. It was a city in constant transition with a geographically mobile population. This anomic, lonely and alienating environment was particularly conducive to the formation and proliferation of working class religious sects – most of which were part of the Holiness movement – which offered some sense of community.[11]

Upon his arrival in Los Angeles, Seymour immediately began to preach at nightly meetings. In addition to the familiar themes of conversion and sanctification, he stressed divine healing, the imminent Second Advent, and glossolalia as a sign accompanying the baptism of the Holy Spirit. Seymour had not yet spoken in tongues himself but he believed it to be an evidence of a person having received the Holy Spirit. Most of his hearers had until then considered sanctification and the baptism of the Holy Spirit to be synonymous. Seymour now made a distinction between them which meant that although his hearers may have been sanctified by the Spirit, they had not yet received the Spirit's baptism.

While some responded favourably to Seymour's preaching on glossolalia, others doubted or rejected it.[12] After his Sunday morning sermon on tongues as the evidence of Spirit baptism at the Holiness Mission on Sante Fe Street, Seymour was invited to lunch at the home of Edward ('Irish') S. Lee and his wife. Returning to the mission for the evening service, he found that the doors had been locked against him by Julia W. Hutchins who announced that she could not allow such extreme teaching.

Seymour returned to the home of Mr and Mrs Lee where he began a solitary vigil of prayer and fasting. Some days later the Lees joined him in prayer and members of the Mission began to visit the house.[13]

In February 1906, Seymour moved into the home of another black couple. Richard and Ruth Asbery, at 214 North Bonnie Brae Street. There, regular prayer meetings were held and the group began to seek the baptism of the Holy Spirit with a sign of glossolalia. On Friday the 6 April they began a ten-day fast. Three days later, Lee asked Seymour to come and pray for his recovery from illness so that he could attend the Monday evening meeting at Bonnie Brae. After anointing with oil and prayer, Lee felt better and requested that Seymour pray for him to receive the Holy Spirit with the sign of tongues.[14] 'Once more', writes Nelson, 'Seymour laid on hands. As he prayed Lee burst forth into rhapsodical utterance in a new tongue. ... 'At last', exulted Lee, 'This is that'.'[15] The two of them walked to the prayer meeting in the nearby Asbery home that evening. The house was crowded with black people, most of whom held menial occupations. No white people were in attendance. After a time of singing, prayer and testifying, Seymour rose to preach on Acts 2:4. He began by recounting the events which had taken place earlier that evening but was unable to proceed further, for as soon as his description of Lee's experience was complete, Lee lifted up his hands and began to speak in other tongues. Nelson describes the scene which followed:

The entire company was immediately swept to its knees as by some tremendous power. At least seven – and perhaps more – lifted their voices in an awesome harmony of strange new tongues. Jennie Evans Moore, falling to her knees from the piano seat, became the first woman thus to speak. Some rushed out to the front porch, yard, and street, shouting and speaking in tongues for all the neighbourhood to hear. ... Teenager Bud Traynor stood on the front porch prophesying and preaching. Jennie Evans Moore returned to the piano and began singing in her beautiful voice what was thought to be a series of six languages with interpretations.[16]

The group believed that this was the restoration of Pentecost.

At this time all the congregation were black and the Asbery's home in which they met was in a black residential district. However, during the following three days crowds gathered and many whites also came as people continued to manifest glossolalia, fall into trances and receive healing. The group quickly became a movement as more and more people came to seek their own Pentecost.[17]

On 12 April Seymour received his Pentecost. Praying late into the night after others were too tired to continue, Seymour and one other, a white man, continued their vigil. Nelson describes what happened:

Finally, the white friend faltered, exhausted. "It is not the time," he said wearily. "Yes it is," replied Seymour, "I am not going to give up." He kept on, alone, and in response to his last prayer, a sphere of white hot brilliance seemed to appear, draw near, and fall upon him. Divine love melted his heart; he sank to the floor seemingly unconscious. Words of deep healing and encouragement spoke to him. As from a great distance he heard unutterable words being uttered – was it angelic adoration and praise? Slowly he realised the indescribably lovely language belonged to him, pouring from his innermost being. A broad smile wreathed his face. At last, he arose and happily embraced those around him.[18]

THE AZUSA STREET MISSION

The new movement rapidly outgrew the Asbery home and larger premises were leased in a run-down area of town at 312 Azusa

Street. Originally a two-storey wooden chapel built in 1888 by the African Methodist Episcopal Church, it was now used to store construction materials. The building was cleared, sawdust scattered on the dirt floor and seating fabricated by laying planks across nail kegs, boxes and odd chairs. The pulpit was constructed from two wooden crates covered with cloth.[19]

Nelson considers, with good reason, that the seating arrangements were significant. Seymour located the pulpit in the centre and formed the pews into 'a circle surrounding the pulpit and altar – all on one level'. This plan, says Nelson,

> ... reflected the *oneness in equality* Seymour envisioned. Worshippers gathered in a new way completely equal in the house of God, the body of Christ not a collection of individuals looking over the back of many heads simply to the clergy or choir but an intimate whole serving one another. This unconventional seating plan revealed Seymour's conviction that events transpiring at Azusa Mission were different, unique, and revolutionary.[20]

The front page of the first edition of the Azusa Mission's newspaper, *The Apostolic Faith* declared that the Pentecostal movement was: '... drawing all together in one body of love, one church, one body of Christ'.[21] News of the events taking place at Bonnie Brae Street and the Azusa mission spread like wildfire through Los Angeles. The 'Los Angeles Times' fanned the flames with their sensational reporting on what was taking place. On the same day as the great San Francisco earthquake and fire, when tremors were felt in Los Angeles, the Times reported that at the Azusa Mission a '... speaker had a vision in which he saw the people of Los Angeles flocking in a mighty stream to perdition. He prophesied awful destruction to this city unless its citizens are brought to a belief in the tenets of the new faith'.[22] The intinerant evangelist, Frank Bartleman, who had settled in Los Angeles in 1904, distributed 75 000 tracts declaring that the earthquake was God's warning. Each day at the Azusa Mission there were three services which often overlapped. Some meetings only attracted about a dozen people but within a month Sunday attendance had risen to seven hundred and fifty or eight hundred with a further four or five hundred, for whom there was no room, standing outside.[23]

The first issue of *The Apostolic Faith* reported that:

Proud, well-dressed preachers came to 'investigate'. Soon their high looks were replaced with wonder, then conviction comes, and very often you will find them in a short time wallowing on the dirty floor, asking God to forgive them and make them as little children.[24]

Nelson declares that: '... multitudes converged on Azusa including virtually every race, nationality, and social class on earth, for Los Angeles contained the world in miniature. ... Never in history had any such group surged into the church of a black person'.[25]

That black and white worshipped together without segregation was in itself unusual in the United States at that time. That this happened under the leadership of a black minister was truly remarkable. For Seymour, the baptism of the Holy Spirit was much more than a glossolalic experience, it was the fulfilment of Joel's prophecy that once again the barriers between the races would be broken down by the coming of the Spirit as on Pentecost. 'The Apostolic Faith' of September 1906 stated that: '... multitudes have come. God makes no difference in nationality. Ethiopians, Chinese, Indians, Mexicans, and other nationalities worship together'.[26] The December issue continued this theme: 'The people are all melted together ... made one lump, one bread, all one body in Christ Jesus. There is no Jew or Gentile, bond or free, in the Azusa Mission. ... He is no respecter of persons or places.'[27] Mack E. Jones, who received the baptism of the Spirit at the Azusa Mission in June 1906, recalled that: 'In Los Angeles he [Seymour] had his meeting, everybody went to the altar together. White and colored, no discrimination seemed to be among them.'[28]

The barriers of sex were also demolished by the Pentecostal outpouring of the Spirit:

Before Jesus ... organised His church, He called them all into the upper room, both men and women, and anointed them with the oil of the Holy Ghost, thus qualifying them all to minister in this Gospel. On the Day of Pentecost they all preached through the power of the Holy Ghost. In Christ Jesus there is neither male nor female, all are one.[29]

Visiting from England, A. A. Boddy, an Anglican clergyman who was to become a leader in the British Pentecostal Movement recorded:

It was something very extraordinary, that white pastors from the South were eagerly prepared to go to Los Angeles to the Negroes, to have fellowship with them and to receive through their prayers and intercessions the blessing of the Spirit. And it was still more wonderful that these white pastors went back to the South and reported to the members of their congregations that they had been together with Negroes, that they had prayed in one Spirit and received the same blessings as they.[30]

Mattie Cummings reported that at Azusa: 'Everybody was just the same, it did not matter if you were black, white, green or grizzly. There was a wonderful spirit. Germans and Jews, black and whites, ate together in the little cottage at the rear. Nobody ever thought of color.[31] When the congregation at Azusa Street organised itself into the Apostolic Faith Gospel Mission, the twelve elders comprised three blacks and nine whites of which five were men and seven women. The barriers of race and sex had been broken down in the pulpit as well as the pew.[32]

In spite of the rundown location of the unimposing Azusa Mission, and the lack of those things – choirs, advertising, financial support and so on – which were normally associated with American revivalism, the movement grew at a phenomenal rate. The Pentecostal message was spread among other church groups including the Armenian church in Los Angeles which already had a history of glossolalia.[33]

THE SPREADING FLAME

Founded in September 1906, the Azusa Mission newspaper, 'The Apostolic Faith', increased from 5000 to 50 000copies by May 1908.[34] So many missionaries went out from Azusa (some thirty-eight left by October 1906)[35] that within two years the movement had spread to over fifty nations including Britain, Scandinavia, Germany, Holland, Egypt, Syria, Palestine, South Africa, Hong Kong, China, Ceylon and India.[36] Christian leaders visited from all over the United States, Canada and the world. Thomas Ball Barratt from Norway and A. A. Boddy from England became leaders of the Pentecostal movement in their respective countries.[37]

Pentecostalism quickly spread to the Southern States. G. B.

Cashwell, a former Methodist minister who had joined the Pentecostal Holiness Church in 1903, arrived at Azusa in November 1906. As a white Southerner his initial reactions were conditioned by his deep rooted anti-black prejudices, but after several days he 'lost his pride' and asked Seymour and several other Negroes to lay hands on him that he might be filled with the Spirit. Shortly after this, he 'began to speak in tongues and praise God' as he was 'filled ... with His Spirit and love'.[38]

On the last day of December 1906 Cashwell brought the Pentecostal message to the white Holiness groups in the South. By 1911 the Pentecostal Holiness Church and the Fire Baptised Holiness Church had merged to form a single Pentecostal organisation under the name of the former. Four years later the Tabernacle Pentecostal Church of South Carolina also merged with the Pentecostal Holiness Church.[39]

In June 1907, Ambrose Jessup Tomlinson, General Overseer of the Church of God (Cleveland) came in contact with the Pentecostal message at Birmingham, Alabama, through the preaching of M. M. Pinson. Throughout 1906 there was increasing interest in the baptism of the Holy Spirit and several Church of God ministers received the experience. In January 1908 Cashwell preached to a congregation in Cleveland which included Tomlinson. Tomlinson 'slipped off' his 'chair in a heap ... at ... Cashwell's feet' and 'spoke in tongues as the Spirit gave the utterance'. From this time the Church of God became Pentecostal.[40]

In Memphis, the leaders of the black Church of God in Christ – C. H. Mason and C. P. Jones – heard of the events taking place in Los Angeles. In March 1907, Mason and two other black ministers travelled to Los Angeles to visit the Azusa Mission. Five weeks later they returned to Memphis having spoken in tongues and become convinced Pentecostals, only to find that the Pentecostal message and experience had preceded them in the person of the white preacher Glen A. Cook. Mason and Cook spread the Pentecostal doctrine which in August 1907 led to a split between the Mason-led Pentecostal faction and the Jones-led non-Pentecostal faction of the Church of God in Christ. The non-Pentecostals expelled Mason and the majority of the ministers and members who retained the name 'Church of God in Christ' and the doctrine of sanctification but added the Pentecostal experience to their articles of faith. Jones remained leader of the non-Pentecostal faction and changed the name to 'The Church of Christ (Holiness) USA'.

The Church of God in Christ with its new Pentecostal emphasis grew rapidly to become the largest Pentecostal group in the United States and the largest black Pentecostal organisation in the world.[41] Many white Pentecostal ministers were ordained by Mason but rather than the Church of God in Christ becoming genuinely interracial, this was largely a matter of convenience for the whites who needed to be ordained by a legally incorporated church organisation in order to obtain cheap travel on the railways and perform weddings. Like Seymour and Parham, these Southern groups retained their doctrine of the 'second work of grace' when they became Pentecostal.

In Los Angeles all the local Pentecostal pastors met with Seymour at the Azusa Mission on a weekly basis, and in the summer of 1907 all the missions united with Azusa for the first Pentecostal camp meeting. In the Spring of the same year the Azusa congregation made a down payment on the Mission and completed the purchase by the following year having raised the total sum of $15 000.[42]

In only two years, [writes Nelson] a small black prayer meeting exploded to take root in fifty nations worldwide. Missionaries with glowing morale were both coming and going literally in every direction. Some arrived from as far away as China to find fulfilment at Azusa before returning with new dedication. Not only had poor drunkards and dope addicts found salvation but learned clergy and veteran missionaries embraced the movement. Seymour glimpsed the potential still ahead, saying, "We are on the verge of the greatest miracle the world has ever seen".[43]

On the 13 May 1908 Seymour quietly married Jennie Evans Moore. Immediately, a small but influential group at the Mission began to criticise him. Clara Lum, Mission Secretary and administrative helper for the newspaper, disapproved of the marriage and immediately left the Mission for Portland, Oregon. With her went the mailing lists for the newspaper (except for the Los Angeles area) which she used to publish it from Portland. Not until a year later did Lum explain anything to the readers.[44]

Without the national and international mailing lists, it was impossible for Seymour to continue publishing. Nelson states that: 'With the passing of the newspaper from Seymour and the Azusa Mission an era ended at Los Angeles. The Pentecostal movement changed decisively from one of interracial equality characterised by unity to one of white domination separated into divisions.'[45]

6 The Redrawing of the Colour Line

Authentic liberation can never occur apart from genuine pentecostal encounter (i.e. the presence of the Spirit), and likewise, authentic pentecostal encounter does not occur without liberation. No man can genuinely experience the fulness of the Spirit and remain a bona fida racist. This was demonstrated during the early pentecostal movement.

Leonard Lovett

In October 1906, Parham had travelled to Los Angeles having received a letter from Seymour and reports from friends who were critical of black influence at the Azusa Mission. With his desire to dominate the movement and ensure that blacks 'kept their place', Parham was strongly opposed to 'white people imitating', what he referred to as, 'the unintelligent, crude negroisms of the Southland, and laying it on the Holy Ghost'.[1] 'When he reached Azusa,' writes Nelson, 'he recoiled in disgust at what he saw: black and whites intermingling against every accepted custom of American society.' 'To my utter surprise and astonishment,' wrote Parham, 'I found conditions even worse than I had anticipated.'[2]

Black and white were worshipping God together and whites were engaging in the same motor behaviour as blacks: shaking, jerking, dancing, falling down and speaking in tongues 'under the power' of the Holy Spirit. Parham went to the pulpit and began to rebuke the worshippers for what he described as 'animalism'. Following a reference to Los Angeles, he later wrote: 'I have seen meetings where all crowded together around the altar, and laying across one another like hogs, blacks and whites mingling; this should be enough to bring a blush of shame to devils, let alone angels, and yet all this was charged to the Holy Spirit.'[3]

The Azusa congregation rejected Parham's racism and claim to leadership and he withdrew to run a rival campaign which lasted until December when he left Los Angeles. During his time in Los Angeles and in his subsequent writings, he continued to criticise and vilify the Azusa Mission and to condemn racial integration.

Parham taught that God's final act on the sixth day of creation – each day of which was an age or a thousand years long – was to create *ex nihilo* a dominant race of men in His image. These were 'the Sons of God'. After resting for a thousand years Sabbath, God 'formed from the earth' an Adamic race on the eighth day. After Adam's son Cain killed his brother Abel, he fled and took a wife from among the 'Sons of God'. 'Thus began', writes Parham,

> the woeful inter-marriage of races for which cause the flood was sent in punishment, and has ever been followed by plagues and incurable diseases upon the third and fourth generation, the offspring of such marriages. Were time to last and inter-marriage continue between the whites, the blacks, and the reds in America, consumption and other diseases would soon wipe the mixed bloods off the face of the earth.[4]

Noah was chosen to be saved from the deluge on the basis of his 'pedigree without mixed blood in it'.[5] The flood destroyed both races, and from Noah's descendants came the Patriarchs of Israel from whom, according to Parham, the 'Aryan race' of Anglo-Saxons are descended. These were the very Saxons – 'Isaac's sons' – who populated Britain, later colonised the United States and of whom Parham was a member. 'Today,' wrote Parham,

> the descendants of Abraham are the Hindus, the Japanese, the high Germans, the Danes (tribe of Dan) the Scandinavians, the Anglo-Saxons and their descendants in all parts of the world. These are the nations who have acquired and retained experimental salvation and deep spiritual truths; while the Gentiles, – the Russians, the Greek, the Italian, the low German, the French, the Spanish and their descendants in all parts are formalists, scarce ever obtaining the knowledge and truth discovered by Luther – that of justification by faith or the truth taught by Wesley, sanctification by faith; while the heathen, – the Black race, the Brown race, the Red race, the Yellow race, in spite of missionary zeal and effort are nearly all heathen still; but will, in the dawning of the coming age be given to Jesus for an inheritance.

Before the eschaton, according to Parham, the Anglo-Saxons are to dominate the other races. 'It is a fact of history', he wrote, 'that the Anglo-Saxon race have and are pushing the nations of Asia, Australia, Africa and America to the ends [of the earth] ... and possessing them, yet they do have their general good will [sic!].'[6]

Following Parham's rejection and condemnation of what was happening at the Azusa Mission, Seymour carefully avoided any form of personal criticism while refuting some of Parham's teachings, particularly his racist views. He wrote in *The Apostolic Faith* of December 1906: 'We believe that God made Adam in His own image ... We do not believe in any eighth day creation, as some have taught, and we do not believe in the annihilation of the wicked.'[7]

When Parham arrived back in Texas he was charged with homosexuality and subsequently went off to look for Noah's Ark.[8] During the mid 1920s he was writing for a racist, anti-Semitic periodical and preached for the notorious Ku Klux Klan whom he referred to as 'those splendid men', who, if converted and revived, would 'realise their high ideals for the betterment of mankind'.[9]

Anderson notes that, although leading Pentecostal periodicals were generally critical of the Klan and recommended its avoidance, this was not because of its violent racism but because Christians should not swear oaths or join secret societies.[10]

Late in 1906, Nettie Harwood, a disciple of Holiness preacher Alma White, visited the Azusa Mission and was incensed when she saw black and white kissing each other and a black woman with 'her arms around a white man's neck praying for him'. Elmer Fisher opened the 'Upper Room' Pentecostal mission in Los Angeles and precipitated the first exodus of whites from Azusa.[11]

Although Seymour's influence upon the Pentecostal movement had gone into decline since the loss of the newpaper in 1908, the Azusa Mission continued as an active interracial fellowship. A. W. Frodsham (brother of the British born Pentecostal leader Stanley Frodsham) wrote of it in 1910 or 1911: 'The Mission has not been flourishing of late but now there are signs of abundance of rain, and many are being blessed. Coloured and white folk worship freely together in this meeting place.'[12]

THE 'FINISHED WORK' CONTROVERSY

In 1911, Seymour departed Los Angeles on a preaching tour, leaving the Mission in the charge of two young black men. While he was away, the ex-baptist William H. Durham – who had visited the Azusa Mission in 1907 – arrived in Los Angeles with his family and a retinue of five helpers. Durham was dogmatically propagating a controversial doctrine which he referred to as 'The Finished Work of Calvary'.[13] He opposed the Wesleyan–Holiness view of sanctification as a second work of grace following conversion, and maintained that the work of sanctification takes place at the same time as justification: when a person is converted.[14]

In February 1911, having been denied the use of the Upper Room, now Los Angeles' largest Pentecostal mission, Durham and his colleagues obtained Azusa for their campaign. For some ten weeks Durham preached at Azusa Street, attracting capacity crowds and dividing the Pentecostal movement in Los Angeles.[15] Such was the controversy that the Azusa trustees contacted Seymour who returned to Los Angeles to find that 'a team of whites from Chicago had for all practical purposes taken over Azusa Mission for the purpose of aggressively preaching a divisive viewpoint'.[16] Seymour insisted that Durham cease to propagate his teaching at Azusa. Durham refused and Seymour padlocked the doors of the Mission against him.

Durham continued to preach his 'Finished Work' doctrine in Los Angeles, Portland and Chicago. Returning to Los Angeles in July 1912, he died of pulmonary tuberculosis. His contentious and sectarian views had by this time split the Pentecostal movement. On the question of sanctification there was no room for dialogue. He condemned and ridiculed the beliefs of his opponents. Glossolalia was for him the only evidence of a person having received the Holy Spirit. Seymour, on the other hand, while accepting glossolalia as the initial evidence, believed it to be but one of the manifestations of the Spirit. While Seymour consistently sought for a multi-racial movement, Durham rejected him and formed a movement dominated by whites.

For Seymour, the love of God was to be demonstrated in unity across the boundaries of colour and gender, while for Durham this was unimportant. Durham rejected Seymour's ecumenism and style of leadership and sought to set himself up as leader of a

movement based on conformity to his own narrow
sectarianism.[17]

The predominantly white northern section of the Pacific Coast
Apostolic Faith Movement broke away from Seymour, accusing
him of rejecting the Second Work teaching on sanctification
while, ironically, most of the white members of the Azusa
Mission left him for rejecting the Finished Work teaching.[18]

All of the white Pentecostal leaders sooner or later separated
themselves from Seymour and Azusa. Their rationalisations for
doing so varied as did the time of their leaving, but ultimately
the whites split away from Seymour and their black religious
origins, and Seymour's dream of equality and interracial
fellowship was left in tatters.[19] As Nelson says: 'Parham
repudiated Seymour's fellowship, Lum took his newspaper.
Durham occupied his building: each one scorned Seymour's
leadership and dismissed the revolutionary new body of equal
believers.'[20]

Durham's followers consolidated the Finished Work wing of
the movement by holding a 'World-Wide Camp Meeting' at Los
Angeles in 1913. It attracted about a thousand people and as
many as two hundred ministers occupied the platform at one
time. Although Seymour attended he was never asked to
participate nor granted any recognition. In April of the
following year, at the instigation of Howard A. Goss and leading
members of the white wing of the Church of God in Christ, a
Finished Work dominated convention was held at Hot Springs,
Arkansas. Several hundred Pentecostals attended of which sixty
eight signed the charter of incorporation of a new white
organisation: the Assemblies of God (AoG). Synan states that:
'As far as is known, no Negroes were invited to the
convention.'[21]

Not only did the Assemblies of God reject the Wesleyan–
Holiness view of sanctification, they also adopted a congregational form of church government rather than the episcopal forms
which the Southern Pentecostals had retained from their
Wesleyan–Holiness origins.

Synan writes that the formation of the Assemblies of God: '...
represented the end of a notable experiment in interracial church
development. After 1914 the Church of God in Christ became
exclusively black while the Assemblies of God continued as a
predominantly white church'.[22]

By the end of the 1920's three out of every five Pentecostals subscribed to the Finished Work view of sanctification.[23] Not only did this doctrinal controversy reflect the division of black from white in the Church of God in Christ and Assemblies of God but the split tended to go through the whole Pentecostal movement. Anderson's research had revealed that:

> The Finished Work movement proved far more attractive to whites than blacks. While two of every three white Pentecostals became Finished Work believers, only one in eight blacks did so. As a consequence, the proportion of blacks in the Finished Work camp was very much less than that in the Second Work wing; about seven percent as compared to thirty percent.[24]

Over two-thirds of the Finished Work Pentecostals lived in urban areas as compared with just over one third of their Second Work counterparts. Those black people who did join the Finished Work wing were even more urban. About nine out of every ten lived in urban areas as compared to about three out of every five among Second Work blacks. In the rural–agrarian South, the majority of Pentecostals remained in the Second Work wing, with less than a quarter embracing the Finished Work teaching.[25]

Ethnic origin was not the only cause of division. Schisms were usually justified or rationalised in terms of geographical location or doctrinal issues. Those from a more Reformed background[26] had fewer reservations about accepting the Finished Work view than they had about the Wesleyan Armenian Second Work position which was more acceptable to those from a Methodist, Holiness or Free Will Baptist tradition.[27]

The split between the Second Work and Finished Work Pentecostals was both racial, geographical and theological. And no doubt personal power struggles played their part in creating divisions. Anderson summarises the causes:

> The Finished Work wing was predominantly Northern and Western, overwhelmingly white, considerably more urban, and reflected the Keswick Holiness backgrounds of its leaders in doctrine and polity. The Second Work wing, on the other hand, was largely Southern, had a very substantial black

minority and was hardly more urban than rural, while its doctrine and polity mirrored the Armenian and Wesleyan Holiness origins of its leadership.[28]

THE SOUTHERN STATES

Not only was colour a significant factor in the split over the Finished Work teaching, it was the central and in some cases the sole reason for one division after another in every section of the Pentecostal movement. In the Southern states the already segregated churches were but fleetingly touched by the message of a Pentecostal experience which transcended race and colour. As early as 1907 when the Fire Baptised Holiness Church became involved with the Pentecostal movement, there was a split which resulted in its black members leaving to form themselves into the Fire Baptised Holiness Church of God. Four years later, the white faction united with the interracial Pentecostal Holiness Church of North Carolina to form the Pentecostal Holiness Church. 'Within two years', writes Anderson, 'the blacks within the new denomination were voted out by the white majority.'[29]

The Church of God (Cleveland) – which originated among the poor white agrarians in the mountains of North Carolina and Tennessee – simply conformed to the racist mores of Southern society.

> From 1909 onwards [writes Church of God historian Charles W. Conn] the Church of God had Negro members and ministers in its fellowship. . . . Barr the earliest black minister, was licensed in 1909 and ordained on June 3, 1912. Almost immediately there were others; the first official register of ministers in the January 1913 'Minutes' included eleven black ministers. . . . in 1913 a black congregation was established in a Tennessee community . . .[30]

On 4 June 1912, Ambrose Jessup Tomlinson, General Overseer of the Church of God, wrote in his diary: 'Had a conference yesterday to consider the question of ordaining Edmund Barr (colored) and setting the colored people off to work among themselves on account of the race prejudice in the South.'[31]

By 1915 the number of black congregations in Florida had increased to nine and Edmund (or Edward) S. Barr was appointed as their overseer. However, after two years the Negro congregations were once again brought under white supervision. Not only did the Church of God conform to the segregationist philosophy of the Southern churches, which resulted in black people worshipping in different congregations than whites, but black congregations were also separated into their own annual Assembly. Cone somewhat euphemistically writes of the 'problems' associated with racial heterogeneity: 'Despite the early interracial idealism of the church, the inescapable mores of the South, with its severe lines of demarcation, had a negative effect on black expansion.'[32] Cone, like so many other white Pentecostal historians, blames the 'mores of the South'; never the racism of white Christians!

In 1921 the apartheid which already existed in Florida was extended to the whole organisation. The black congregations were reorganised under their own black overseer, and for the next four years the only contact between the black and white factions consisted of the attendance of the black and white overseers at each others segregated annual Assemblies. Tomlinson, while stating: 'I do not like any separations between nationalities and races', sought to justify it by arguing that, 'it is not always convenient, neither is it best, for different races to meet together regularly for worship'.[33]

A resolution was adopted in 1926, stipulating that the General Overseer of the black congregations always be a white man, and allowing them to send delegates to the white annual Assembly. Few did.[34]

Thus, the white dominated Church of God who were so willing to suffer persecution for the sake of doctrine, conformed without any visible resistance to the racism of the South, and even ensured the continued domination of blacks by whites in their organisation.

THE DEATH OF SEYMOUR AND THE END OF AZUSA

Durham had taken some two-thirds of Seymour's stafff with him following the Finished Work controversy, and subsequently meetings at the Azusa Mission dropped to one a week: all day

Sunday. At the end, the congregation had fallen to about twenty people who were largely the original group from Bonnie Brae Street plus six to eight white people, most of whom were women. Offerings fell so low that sometimes Seymour would have to ask the congregation for enough to cover the expenses. The theological divisions and power struggles within the movement, which had reflected, justified or at least paralleled the racial divisions, left Seymour and the Azusa Mission bereft of recognition or support.[35]

In 1914 Seymour revised the Azusa Mission's 'Articles of Incorporation' and 'Constitution' to read that: '... the Apostolic Faith Mission ... should be carried on in the interests of and for the benefit of the colored people of the State of California, but the people of all countries, climes, and nations shall be welcome.'[36] And that the Bishop, Vice-Bishop and Trustees were to be 'people of color'.[37] Seymour continued to believe that all races should be united by their common faith in Christ and shared experience of the baptism of the Holy Spirit, but his treatment at the hands of many white Pentecostals led him to ensure that Azusa was not taken over by those who would once again keep the black man outside the door and bar him from the altar. 'Our colored brethren,' he wrote, 'must love our white brethren and respect them in the truth so that the word of God can have its free course, and out white brethren must love their colored brethren and respect them in the truth so that the Holy Spirit won't be grieved.'[38] On the 28th September, 1922 Bishop William Joseph Seymour died, aged 52. His followers said that he died of a broken heart 'overwhelmed,' writes Nelson, 'with sorrow, grief, or disappointment.'[39]

In 1938 the bank foreclosed on a loan made to Mrs. Seymour and took possession of the Azusa Mission. Later it was demolished and the land made into a car park. An ignominious end for the cradle of the now world-wide Pentecostal and Charismatic movements.

THE 'NEW ISSUE' CONTROVERSY

The second major split in the Pentecostal movement – which however mainly affected the Finished Work wing – was precipitated by what became known as the 'New Issue', 'Jesus only', 'Jesus name' or 'Oneness' controversy. This originally began as a debate – mainly within the Assemblies of God – on the correct formula to be used when water baptism was administered. The Oneness (or Apostolic) Pentecostals claimed that the command in Matthew 28:19 meant that candidates should be baptised using the simple formula as recorded in the Acts of the Apostles: 'in the name of Jesus' only rather than in the 'titles' Father, Son and Holy Ghost.[40] This rapidly developed into controversy over the nature of the Godhead, with the Oneness Pentecostals espousing a modalistic teaching while the others became all the more deeply entrenched in trinitarianism. Ultimately, the Oneness position identified regeneration – being 'born again' – with water baptism in the name of Jesus Christ and the baptism of the Holy Spirit evidenced by glossolalia.[41] For them, 'full salvation' was dependent upon obedience to the 'three steps' set forth in Acts 2:38: repentance, water baptism and Spirit baptism. This denial of sola fide – salvation through faith alone – distanced the Oneness faction even further, not only from other Pentecostals but also from the rest of orthodox Christianity.[42]

Although both the triadic and the simple formulae had been used by Pentecostals for some time, the simple formula became an issue after a pre-baptismal sermon on the subject was delivered by the Canadian Pentecostal leader Robert E. McAllister at the 'World-Wide Pentecostal Camp Meeting' held at Arroyao Seco, California in April 1913. Also at the camp meeting was John G. Scheppe who, having spent the night in prayer, ran through the camp in the early hours of the morning declaring that God had revealed to him the need for all to be baptised in the name of Jesus.[43] The message of 'baptism in Jesus' name' was taken up by several ministers who attended the camp meeting and subsequently spread 'the revelation' among the Finished Work Pentecostals in and around Los Angeles, the West Coast, the Midwest and the South. Within two years it had become a major issue in the Assemblies of God. Special conferences and articles in Pentecostal periodicals warned against the 'new issue' but to little avail. All the Assemblies of God preachers in Louisiana and many in Texas, Arkansas, and Oklahoma embraced the teaching, as did several of the Assemblies' officials.[44]

At the instigation of J. Roswell Flower and others, steps were taken to remove those who were sympathetic to Jesus' name baptism from positions of authority, and ultimately to expel the Oneness faction from the Assemblies of God. At the Assemblies General Council in October 1916, the trinitarians were success-ful in obtaining a majority endorsement for their sixteen point 'Statement of Fundamental Truths', which resulted in the exodus of 156 of their 585 ministers and over a hundred congregations, including all the advocates of the Oneness doctrines.[45]

The underlying causes of the 'new issue' split were more complex than disagreement over the Oneness doctrines. Although these were clearly important to the protagonists, they were more probably rationalisations for schism than genuine reasons. The Assemblies had beens severely criticised by the mainline denominations for – among other things – their fellowship with black Christians. Under this onslaught from racist white evangelicals – coupled with desire of the Assemblies of God to become 'respectable' – the white leadership was only too willing to purge their organisation of those who caused 'offence'. Furthermore, one suspects that the removal of the Oneness 'heretics', which resulted in the loss of black ministers and congregations, was not an unwelcome or unforseen consequence.

There is also evidence that the Flower faction within the Assemblies – which had come from the white section of the Church of God in Christ – utilised opposition to the 'new issue' to remove from positions of power, not only advocates of, or sympathisers with the Oneness doctrines, but also those who were not part of the Flower caucus. As things worked however, the Flower faction also lost their positions of authority within the movement.[46]

At the 1916 General Council meeting which resulted in the withdrawal of the 'Jesus only' faction, Garfield Thomas Haywood, one of the most influential black advocates of the Oneness position and pastor of a large predominantly black yet interracial congregation in Indianapolis, was singled out for personal derision and abuse. One speaker for the trinitarian side referred to the 'new issue' doctrines as 'hay, wood, and stubble and in an allusion to Haywood's periodical, 'A Voice Crying in the Wilderness', mocked that 'they are all in the wilderness and they have a voice in the wilderness'.[47] 'Following the Oneness schism', writes Anderson,

> the Assemblies became an all but 'lily white' denomination. ... could it have been that racial animosities had contributed ever so slightly, to the turn of the tide? Was the emergence of the Assemblies as a de facto 'lily white' denomination a wholly unanticipated or unwelcome consequence of the doctrinal struggle? Since 1916, except for a few black faces here and there in urban congregations in the Northeast, the Assemblies has remained a white man's church.[48]

THE PENTECOSTAL ASSEMBLIES OF THE WORLD

Many of those who withdrew from the Assemblies of God over the 'new issue' controversy sought for some way of bringing about cooperation and coordination in the infant Oneness movement. In 1906 an organisation called the Pentecostal Assemblies of the World (PA of W) had been formed in Los Angeles.[49] Among its early leaders were J.J. Frazee, who became General Superintendent in 1912, and G.T. Haywood the most outstanding and influential of the black Oneness leaders.[50] Haywood claimed to have been a minister with the Pentecostal Assemblies of the World since 1911.[51] Although at its inception it was not distinctively a Oneness organisation, it became so in 1918.

At the end of December and beginning of January 1916–17, many of the Oneness ministers who had just left the Assemblies of God two months earlier met together at Eureka Springs, Arkansas to form the General Assembly of the Apostolic Assemblies.[52] On 6 April 1917, the United States entered the First World War and the Apostolic Assemblies, because they were not recognised by the Clergy Bureau, were faced with the problem of their younger ministers being called up for military service. A further difficulty caused by this lack of recognition involved their ministers being refused the concessionary rate for travel on the railways. The solution was to find a recognised organisation with which they could arrange a merger. Such a group was the Pentecostal Assemblies of the World. However, as with many other 'marriages of convenience', the relationship was to be short-lived.[53]

In January 1918 the two organisations met together at St. Louis, Missouri and became a single body under the name 'Pentecostal Assemblies of the World'. At this meeting J.J. Frazee held the office of General Superintendent and Chairman, D. C. Opperman, the former chairman of the Apostolic Assemblies was elected as Secretary and H. A. Goss became Treasurer. In October of the same year, another convention was held and the chairmanship passed to E. W. Doak (white) and the office of Secretary to W. E. Booth-Clibborn (white). From this time, several prominent individuals in the Pentecostal Assemblies disappear from the records, including the original founder of the organisation J.J. Frazee.[54] Arthur L. Clanton writes of this meeting that: '... few if any Negro ministers were present, and very little business was transacted'.[55]

In January 1919, a further meeting was held and the office of Secretary passed from Booth-Clibborn (white) to G. T. Haywood (black). Four out of the twenty-one Field Superintendents who had been listed in January 1918 were black – one of these was Haywood – and by January 1919 some of the names of white ministers disappeared and those of black ministers increased. The only committee to be formed during the convention of 1919 was composed of seven men of whom at least two were black and when, several days later, the Pentecostal Assemblies of the World was incorporated as a 'voluntary association' in the state of Indiana, the incorporators and board of directors were the white ministers, Edward W. Doak and Daniel C. Opperman, and the black minister Garfield T. Haywood. Fred J. Foster wrote in his *History of the Oneness Movement* that: 'This was to prove a unique fellowship for several years, because both white and colored were members.'[56] The Pentecostal Assemblies was developing from a multi-racial but predominantly white organisation to one in which both black and white were working together and, more importantly, sharing in leadership.[57]

The white Southern minister, S. C. McClain, who had left the Assemblies of God over the 'new issue', was a founding member of the Apostolic Assemblies and had taken part in the merger with the Pentecostal Assemblies of the World. In 1918 he wrote of his experiences in this multiracial organisation.

I was from the South, where it had been considered improper

for a white person to have equal fellowship with, or sit at table with, Colored people. My wife who had been raised in Indianapolis, thought nothing of these things. I asked her, "Do we shake hands with Colored people?" Her answer was, "Most certainly we do!" After I got used to it, I thought it was wonderful. I thought nothing of the color line.[58] Throughout the north and east there seemed to be very little, if any, race prejudice. I, being southern born, thought it a miracle that I could sit in a service by a colored saint of God and worship, or eat at a great camp table, and forget I was eating beside a colored saint, but in spirit and truth God was worshipped in love and harmony.[59]

The 'love and harmony' was soon to be replaced by acrimony, and the 'miracle' overthrown by the re-drawing of the colour line through the Oneness movement. Pentecostal Assemblies of the World historian, Morris E. Golder writes:

As the history of the organisation moves forward, a change that can hardly go unnoticed has taken place. At the beginning of the P.A. of W., the organisation in the main was made up of white brethren. There was no distinction made as to color in the beginning; for ... the outpouring of the Spirit of God wiped away ALL racial barriers. However, the more the brethren moved out of the realm of the spiritual into that of the natural, color did become not only an issue, but a 'divise issue' at that ...[60]

During the years 1920 and 1921 the number of black ministers joining the Pentecostal Assemblies of the World steadily increased. Many became officials and members of committees, and of the twenty four 'Executive elders' in 1921, one-third were black.[61]

The increased involvement of black people in the leadership of the PA of W resulted in many racially prejudiced whites leaving. Golder notes that: 'It is evident that as the P.A. of W. became a more integrated organization, the unrest among the white brethren, especially in the South grew in proportion.'[62] In November 1922, the white Oneness Pentecostals in the South held their own segregated 'Southern Bible Conference'.[63] As the PA of W began to disintegrate, attempts were made to hold it together. For the General Assembly which met in October 1923, the 'issue of color and race' was of great importance and it passed resolutions aimed at preventing the organisation 'being rent asunder'.[64] 'Every means available', writes Golder, 'was employed to ward off the schism that eventually came ... [but] The "demon of prejudice" continued to control the minds of many of the brethren, specially the white brethren of the South.[65] A further resolution passed at the 1923 assembly stated that:

> ... because of conditions now existing in many parts of the country through no fault of the brethren, but rather those who oppose the work of the Lord, it is deemed advisable that two white Presbyters sign the credentials for the white brethren (especially in the southland) and two colored Presbyters sign the papers of the colored brethren.[66]

'It was said.' writes Golder, 'that "many of the white brethren in the South were made to suffer because a black man's name appeared in his credentials".' Are we expected to believe that a person's colour is discernible from his signature? Other purported reasons for this legislation were somewhat more honest and clearly reveal the racism of the white schismatics. One such justification asserted that, 'it was never intended that a black brother should be equal with his white brethren even in the Lord'.[67]

In October the following year (1924), at the Annual Convention of the PA of W, the final split came. Earlier in the month the Texas district had met, changed their name to 'The Pentecostal Assemblies of Jesus Christ' and segregated the movement so that 'the white race' and 'the Colored race' came 'under separate managements'.[68] The same proposal was considered during the 1924 convention. W. E. Kidson, a white Oneness minister, wrote that:

> It was the general opinion that this [the problems arising from interracial organisation] was a hinderance to the spreading of the gospel. For several years it had been talked, pro and con, about separation, not on doctrinal lines, but on racial lines. ... During the convention, it was first proposed ... that there be an Eastern and a Western division, the one to be exclusively Colored, and the other exclusively white. ... This proposal was rejected.[69]

Having failed in their attempt to create a segregated organisation, the majority of white ministers met together to set up their own all-white Oneness group called 'The Apostolic Church of Jesus Christ', later renamed 'The Pentecostal Ministerial Alliance'. The following year, two other all white Oneness sects were established – 'Emmanuel's Church in Jesus Christ' and 'The Apostolic Churches of Jesus Christ'. These groups later contracted several mergers with each other and in 1945 came together to form the white United Pentecostal Church.[70]

The 'white' version of the white exodus from the PA of W maintains that '...when the white ministers left the Pentecostal Assemblies of the World, it was not because of racial prejudice on their part'.[71] On the contrary, they argue that it was caused by 'misunderstanding by the younger northern colored ministers of the question of segregation in the South' and by the 'segregation laws' and 'tradition' of the South. McClain wrote that: 'While all Spirit-filled ministers agreed that with God there is not a color line and in the hearts of the people of God there should be none, yet ministers labouring in the South had to conform to laws and customs.'[72] Arthur Clanton, General Superintendent of the United Pentecostal Church, attempted to justify their position when he wrote:

> Southern whites and Negroes did not worship together. Had such been attempted in the South, the result would have been bitter resentment among the white non-Pentecostals. This, in turn, could have seriously handicapped the future ministry of these Southern preachers and their churches.[73]

At best, the majority of white Oneness Pentecostal leaders were spineless in their unwillingness to challenge the racist mores of the South. At worst, they were as prejudiced and bigoted as the majority of whites – both Christian and non-Christian – on both sides of the Mason Dixon line. To their credit, not all of the white ministers left the PA of W. A minority stayed and the Assemblies remained interracial though overwhelmingly black.[74]

In 1931 the Assemblies' Presiding Bishop, G.T. Haywood died and a delegation of white ministers from the Pentecostal Ministerial Alliance (Apostolic Church of Jesus Christ) approached the PA of W with offers of a merger. The merger proposal was accepted, the new organisation named 'The

Pentecostal Assemblies of Jesus Christ' (PA of JC) and the PA of W's 'episcopal' polity replaced with the 'presbyterian' polity of the Pentecostal Ministerial Alliance. It looked as if the dead phoenix of interracial Oneness Pentecostalism was rising from the ashes of American racism. A few of the ministers of the PA of W were sceptical and reorganised the rump of their organisation the following year. Their scepticism was well founded, for the white ministers sought to dominate the PA of JC and in 1937 held their National Meeting in Tulsa, Oklahoma, where blacks could not legally gather with whites. This started an exodus of blacks from the PA of JC back into the PA of W. By 1938 the PA of JC had an all white board of Presbyters.[75]

Thus, the racially integrated Pentecostal movement which was brought to birth among the black Holiness community in Los Angeles was rapidly segregated and conformed to the racist norms of American society and of the American churches. White Pentecostals were unwilling to challenge the racist laws and mores of the United States or to stand up to the criticism of the mainline denominations who sought to discredit them by pointing to their interracial character and black roots.[76] Instead, they yielded to the pressures of segregated American society and the apartheid of American Christianity, and pointed heavenward when challenged on the question of origins. The divisions in the Pentecostal movement were caused by (or justified in terms of) many interrelated factors – disagreements over doctrine, struggles for power and dominance, desire to achieve 'respectability', social diversity and geographical location – but the end result demonstrated that white Pentecostals did not wish to maintain an interracial movement, submit to black leadership or recognise the black origins of their movement.

7 Black Birth, Interracial Infancy, Segregated Childhood

The primary social sources of American denominationalism are to be sought in the European history of the churches which have immigrated to the new world . . . many others . . . owe the development of their separate individuality to the operation of social forces native to the new environment. . . . The third set of social factors which have been responsible for a great deal of denominationalism in America have arisen out of the forced migration to the New World of the African race and out of the subsequent relations of whites and Negroes.

H. Richard Niebuhr

. . . the sincerity of whites who claimed to be in true fellowship with blacks can be challenged because they have refused to defy mores and prejudices by serving under black leaders . . .

Leonard Lovett

BLACK BIRTH

Vinson Synan – a white Pentecostal historian – has noted that black Pentecostals. '. . . often attempt to demonstrate that the pentecostal movement began as a Negro phenomenon, later accepted by whites'.[1] This is certainly the opinion of black Pentecostal, James S. Tinney (1971, 1976, 1979) who asserts that '. . . Pentecostalism, both Black and white, was essentially Black in origin. . .'[2] Leonard Lovett (1973, 1975) another black Pentecostal historian writes:

It may be categorically stated that black pentecostalism emerged out of the context of the brokenness of black existence. Interestingly, William J. Seymour, W. E. Fuller, first overseer of the black wing of the Fire Baptised Holiness Church of the Americas, C. H. Mason, founder of the Church

77

of God in Christ, and G.T. Haywood of the Pentecostal Assemblies of the World, were all the sons of emancipated slaves. Their holistic view of religion had its roots in African religion.[3]

White researchers like Vinson Synan (1961) and Douglas Nelson (1981), while recognising that blacks had an important role in the birth and development of the Pentecostal movement ascribed to it an interracial origin.[4] However, as early as 1965, the Swiss missiologist and scholar of Pentecostalism, Walter Hollenweger recognised that,

> The pentecostal experience of Los Angeles was neither the leading astray of the Church by demons ... nor the eschatological pouring out of the Holy Spirit (as the Pentecostal movement itself claimed) but an outburst of enthusiastic religion of a kind well known and frequent in the history of Negro churches in America which derived its specifically Pentecostal features from Parham's theory that speaking with tongues is a necessary concomitant of the baptism of the Spirit.[5]

Parham's only significant contribution to the movement appears to have been his teaching that glossolalia is the necessary evidence of a person having received the baptism of the Holy Spirit. Seymour on the other hand, while accepting Parham's 'evidence doctrine', did not equate tongues with the Spirit baptism, did not limit the charismata to the nine referred to in 1 Corinthians 12, and in common with other black Christians had a broader and more social view of the power and gifts of the Spirit.[6]

That Hollenweger's assessment is correct is adequately evidenced by two reports of events at the Azusa Mission. Both, though written by detractors, amply illustrate the continuity between West African folk religion, black Christianity and early Pentecostalism. 'The Los Angeles Daily Times' of Wednesday morning, April 18th, 1906, under the headline "Weird Babel of Tongues", described in condemnatory terms the motor behaviour of the worshippers:

> ... the devotees ... work themselves into a state of mad excitement in their peculiar zeal. Colored people and a sprinkling of whites compose the congregation ... worshippers

... spend hours swaying forth and back in a nerve-racking attitude of prayer and supplication ... an old colored 'mammy,' in a frenzy of religious zeal [is] swinging her arms wildly about her ... a bucksome dame was overcome with excitement and almost fainted. Undismayed by the fearful attitude of the colored worshippers, another black women [sic] jumped to the floor and began a wild gesticulation.... The sister continued until it was necessary to assist her to a seat because of her bodily fatigue.[7]

Charles Parham, writing nineteen years after the event, and to some extent motivated by his racist prejudices, declared:

There was a beautiful outpouring of the Holy Spirit in Los Angeles. ... Then they pulled off all the stunts common in old camp meetings among colored folks.... That is the way they worship God, but what makes my soul sick, and make me sick at my stomach is to see white people imitating unintelligent crude negroisms of the Southland, and laying it on the Holy Ghost.[8]

Both sources graphically illustrate that the type of behaviour taking place at Azusa Street was that which was already common in black Christianity and had developed as part of the bi-cultural synthesis which had taken place during slavery.

Not only did the motor behaviour of the participants reveal the early Pentecostal movement's debt to African folk religion, but the leitmotive of black Christianity, which had their origins either in Africa or in slavery, continued to echo in early black inspired Pentecostalism: Spirit possession and spiritual power (accompanied by trances, dreams, prophesying, healing and exorcism); the integration of the seen and unseen worlds; freedom; racial equality; black personhood and dignity; community; and belief in the imminent Second Advent of Christ.

Black people were particularly attracted to the early Pentecostal movement, for not only did it offer the hope of a genuine racial equality and fellowship, but it also echoed these familiar leitmotive. The relevance and integration of religion and the supernatural in all of life and the joyous celebration of life was expressed in forms of liturgy which originated in West Africa. The African desire and respect for spiritual power and belief in Spirit possession was central to the movement. Seymour wrote that: 'The gift of tongues is the glory of God flooding your soul and the Spirit taking possession.'[9] This possession took place to the accompanyment of music, dancing and motor behaviour which was essentially West African in origin. The immanence of God was recognised and the power and presence of God experienced in the liberty of the Spirit. Western literary theology was displaced by the oral theology of the story, the testimony and the song. The early Pentecostal movement was also revolutionary, not only in terms of its ability to transcend the colour line, but also in its adventism. The early Pentecostals anticipated the imminent cataclismic end of the age to be brought about by the Second Advent of Christ. Although God was perceived as the prime mover in this eschatological event, Pentecostals saw themselves as agents of the forthcoming revolution. The arrival of the Kingdom could be hastened by them fulfilling the preconditions for the Lord's return by preaching the gospel in all the world.[10] They believed glossolalia – or more correctly xenoglossia – to be God's means of communicating the message of salvation through them to the heathen of other lands in their native languages. Subsequent experiences forced Pentecostals to accept that the ability to speak in tongues was neither a substitute for the study of languages nor a means of mass evangelism among the heathen.

Believing the Second Advent to be imminent, most of the early Pentecostals used the limited resources at their disposal to propagate the gospel and their distinctive emphasis on the Spirit baptism, rather than to establish permanent congregations. Christian periodicals, the training and support of missionaries, and the holding of camp meetings, conventions and evangelistic campaigns took precedence over spending on the rent or purchase of places of worship. Many missionaries, itinerant preachers and pastors endured severe privations – poverty, hunger and lack of adequate accommodation – as they laboured to spread the gospel and thus hasten the second coming of Christ. Only when this initial expectancy and enthusiasm had abated, and glossolalia been discredited as a means of evangelism, did Pentecostals begion to erect buildings and form denominations.

The early Pentecostal movement in common with its Holiness predecessors, strenuously rejected 'the world'. The dominant secular culture was challenged – often with a vengeance – and a

Pentecostal counter culture established on the basis of a rigid system of ethics and taboos. The dichotomous or naturalistic world view of the West was replaced with the holistic integrated world view of Africa (which was not so different from that of pre-enlightenment Europe). Their God was a God of miracles and a new age, for which they were preparing themselves and the world, was about to dawn.

It is of great significance that the Pentecostal movement was born, not in Parham's Bible school in Topeka, Kansas but at an all black prayer meeting in a black ghetto in Los Angeles. Although Parham's students had experienced glossolalia in January 1901, the spark was quickly extinguished and by 1903 Parham had returned to his original emphasis on divine healing. What occurred on Friday 6 April, 1906 at the home of Richard and Ruth Asbery – and later moved to 312 Azusa Street – was a blaze of spiritual fervour which within two years had spread to more than fifty nations.[11]

Interestingly, the black origins of the movement were recognised by the Dutch Pentecostal leader G. R. Polman. In 1915 Polman wrote to G. A. Wumkers: 'Parham has said that he is the founder of the Pentecostal Movement, but this was a political move by him and later it became apparent that his motives were not right.'[12] Polman also informed him that:

> ... the Pentecostal Movement originated in Los Angeles (1906), in a group of converted coloured people who came together and prayed for the baptism with the Holy Spirit, just as the first disciples received it at the beginning. Their prayers have been answered and today it has spread.[13]

Polman had recognised the Negro origins of the movement and made this clear to the German Pentecostal leaders.[14] In September 1909, the main leaders of the German Evangelical Movement signed the 'Berlin Declaration' in which they castigated Pentecostalism as 'Not from Above but from Below'.[15] Was there an implicit suggestion in this statement that a movement which originated among black people was consequently satanic? The reaction of the German Pentecostals to the criticisms of the Evangelicals was to deny their movement's Negro origins (even though Polman had left them without the excuse of ignorance) and claim a heavenly one.

Only one British writer of this era appears to have recognised and referred to its black roots, and then only as a criticism of the movement. This was Sir Robert Anderson who in 1912 published a pamphlet entitled 'Spirit Manifestations and the Gift of Tongues'.[16]

INTERRACIAL INFANCY

From its black origins, the infant Pentecostal movement rapidly became interracial, and this was in spite of the fact that black people were still generally despised and treated as inferior by white society. Synan notes that:

> ... what began as a local revival in a Negro church became of interest to people all over the nation, regardless of race. In a short while the majority of the attendants were white ...[17]

This striking interracial phenomenon occurred in the very years of America's most racist period, those from 1890 to 1920. In an age of Social Darwinism, Jim Crowism, and general white supremacy, the fact that Negroes and whites worshipped together in virtual equality among the pentecostals was a significant exception to prevailing racial attitudes. Even more significant is the fact that this interracial accord took place among the very groups that had traditionally been most at odds, the poor whites and the poor blacks.[18]

The early Pentecostal movement, in common with the Holiness movement, was largely working class, although the majority of Pentecostals tended to come from the lower working class. Unlike the Holiness movement, however, which had many middle class leaders, the Pentecostal movement in the United States was as proletarian in leadership as it was in membership.[19]

The interracial nature of the Azusa meetings was to a great extent a reflection of Seymour's desire for racial equality. He was committed to the elimination of the colour line, the breaking down of all barriers between black and white and the recognition and living out of true demonstrable equality. For this reason, writes Douglas Nelson, '... he joined the most integrated branch of the Methodist Church – the original champion of American slaves.[20] Still dissatisfied, he moved to Cincinnati and was ordained by what Nelson describes as, '... the most racially integrated church in American life at this time; black and white believers actually mixed together happily in the same building'.[21] Shunning the possibility of forming a black congregation in Houston, Seymour accepted the call to be pastor of the black but pro-integrationist Holiness group in Los Angeles. There both black and white were attracted to his message of Spirit baptism, and although there were no whites present on 6 April 1906, when glossolalia erupted at the home of the Asberys, they arrived soon afterwards. Synan recognises: 'That the one outstanding personality in bringing about the Pentecostal revival in Los Angeles was a Negro is a fact of extreme importance to Pentecostals of all races.'[22] Black Pentecostal, Leonard Lovett goes further and correctly notes: 'Seymour ... apostle of Pentecost, defied the racist mentality of his time and opened the revival to everyone [and this is] a factor of supreme importance in explaining the success of the revival.'[23] 'Seymour', writes Nelson, '... rejected the false gospel of a racial exclusion for the *essential doctrine* of the oneness of the body of Christ.'[24] He reaffirmed what he believed to be 'the original basis for fellowship: human equality in Christ'. Whites and blacks flocked to Azusa where the theory of racial equality became a reality and where, in the words of Frank Bartleman, 'the "color line" was washed away in the blood'. Although whites came to a revival which was led by a Negro and had begun among black people, the meetings at the Mission were 'conducted on the basis of complete racial equality'.[25]

Not only was the Pentecostal movement especially attractive to black Christians because it unashamedly reflected the leitmotive of black religion, but as the mainstream denominations – particularly the Methodist and Baptist – moved away from experiential religion, their black members became increasingly alienated. The Pentecostal movement had what they were looking for: total involvement of mind, body and emotions in unrestrained worship. Synan notes that:

> When the traditional churches began to add more form and decorum to their services, the emotionally inclined Negro gravitated to the pentecostal churches. At least eighty per cent of the members of Negro pentecostal churches came from other churches, particularly from Baptist and Methodist denominations.[26]

Among the Pentecostals, black people were no longer disadvantaged because of their colour or lack of education, for the Spirit could minister through whoever was yielded to Her influence. No longer was the pulpit closed to those lacking seminary training. The Holy Spirit qualified and empowered those whose hearts were converted rather than those whose heads were filled. Here, black and white, the poor and the illiterate – all could share and participate fully in the life and worship of the Pentecostal congregation.

Douglas Nelson is in no doubt as to what attracted people of all races to the Azusa Mission:

> Seymour saw the church as a new body of equals both interracial and glossolalic. Interracial togetherness could be denied only for forsaking the gospel itself – apostacy – while glossolalia meant simply a gift of power upon the unified church body. The cross itself was meant to bring all persons of earth together in a new wholeness beyond divisions of race, sex, nation, or class. The 'apostolic faith' included interracial unity and glossolalic ecstasy producing a happiness and power attractive to vast multitudes of people.[27]

More than anything else, it is likely that people were attracted to Azusa because of the power that was being manifest. Seymour was a 'fatalist' in the sense that Joseph R. Washington uses the term.[28] He looked beyond human effort and ability for a solution to the problems of racial prejudice, discrimination and inequality of treatment. Like his forefathers in the bondage of slavery and his ancestors in West Africa, Seymour sought for power from God to influence the social milieu in which he lived. During the first months of the revival in Los Angeles, the movement under Seymour's leadership emphasised the folly of human effort and the need to rely completely on the power of the Holy Spirit. Robert Mapes Anderson refers to: '... the utter dependance of those at Azusa upon the direct operation of the Spirit. Believing that all human efforts at promotion of the work were antithetical to reliance on the Spirit'.[29] Sarah Covington, who participated in the Azusa revival, recalled that the first three years were characterised by the power of the Spirit, Larry Christenson, who conversed with her, records: 'One word more than any other, interlaces her recounting of those days: *power.*' She states: 'We had *power* in those days, and I haven't seen anything like it since!'[30]

What attracted so many was not a theology of power but an experience of power. Christenson is at least partly correct when he notes that, '... it was not doctrine, but the *event* of speaking in tongues. which midwifed the birth of modern-day Pentecostalism'.[31] However, for Seymour and the early attenders at Azusa, the power of the Spirit was more than glossolalia. Speaking in tongues was only one of the gifts of the Holy Spirit and, although Seymour believed it to be of great importance, he did not accord to it the preeminence given later by white Pentecostals. His newspaper *The Apostolic Faith* declared: 'We preach old-time repentance, old-time conversion, old-time sanctification, and old-time baptism with the Holy Ghost, which is the gift of power upon the sanctified life, and God throws in the gift of tongues.'[32] Certainly Seymour did make a distinction between the 'witness of tongues' which a person received when they were baptised with the Spirit, and the 'gift of tongues' which only some received as a result of Spirit baptism. He wrote: 'You may not receive the gift of tongues when you receive the witness of tongues, that is to say, – you will speak in tongues when you are baptized with the Holy Spirit.'[33] While Seymour clearly accepted Parham's 'evidence doctrine', unlike the majority of white Pentecostals who deserted him, he did not equate glossolalia with the Spirit baptism, nor did he limit the gifts of the Spirit to the nine listed in Paul's Corinthian letter. *The Apostolic Faith'* reported the occurrence of '... the gift of prophecy, and writing in foreign languages ... the gift of writing in unknown languages, also the gift of playing instruments ... visions ... the gift of singing as well as speaking in the inspiration of the Spirit ... trance ... dreams ...' and so on.[34] In answer to the question: 'What is the real evidence that a man or woman has received the baptism with the Holy Ghost?' Seymour himself wrote: 'Divine love which is charity ... and the outward manifestations; speaking in tongues and the signs following: casting out devils, laying hands on the sick and the sick being healed, and the love of God for souls increasing in our hearts.'[35] For Seymour, the evidence had to be more substantial than glossolalia alone. Love and power were to be demonstrated among the Pentecostals. Perhaps most importantly, Seymour believed that the power of the Holy Spirit could bring about a unity between Christians of all races and colours – a view shared by the black Church of God in Christ minister Leonard Lovett who, speaking of the Holy Spirit, declares: 'There is a power in the world that can bridge racial, denominational, national, cultural and class barriers.'[36]

The early Pentecostal movement was attractive to all races because, as Emil Brunner says: 'People draw near to the Christian community because they are invisibly attracted to its supernatural power. They would like to share in this new dimension of life and power ...'.[37] In the United States and in many other nations which had been affected by Enlightenment and post-Enlightenment philosophy – rationalism, humanism, materialism – and social fragmentation, the Pentecostal movement provided a return to the holistic, non-rational, miraculous, supernatural, experiential, emotive, oral, narrative, communitarian and participatory religion which overcomes the alienation which results when man exists in a society or culture which denies essential parts of his being. In this sense, Huibert H. Zegwaart was correct when he stated that: 'There are many roots to Pentecostalism because it is rooted in human experience.'[38] Such a denial of areas of human experience by both secular culture and institutionalised Christianity, made Pentecostalism attractive to vast numbers of people.

The early Pentecostal movement was primarily an event or experience movement rather than an idea or philosophical one. The early Pentecostals were seeking for experiences of pneumatic power. Understanding developed out of the event. The existing theological traditions and systems – including the Wesleyan Holiness perspective – were always more or less inadequate as bases for understanding the baptism and gifts of the Holy Spirit and tended, when adopted by Pentecostals, to limit their understanding and hence their pneumatic experience and the 'freedom' of the Spirit to 'control' the Church. In their attempt to fit the presence and power of the Holy Spirit into existing theological categories, most of the white Pentecostal sects and also – though to a lesser extent – many of the black ones, demanded that the Church 'control' the Spirit and make His manifestations subject to ecclesiastical interdict.[39] Being possessed by the Spirit gave way to possessing the Spirit. The Ruach Yahweh was locked up in individuals and in the emerging white dominated Pentecostal denominations. Ecumenism, racial-heterogenaity and the pneumatic dynamism to effect social change gave way to sectarianism, racial homogeneity and the incestuous quest for personal purity. The inability or unwillingness of the Pentecostal movement to produce a pneumatology of its own, and its adoption of existing, and hence inadequate, understandings of the Spirit have resulted in a loss of dynamism and relevance in the white dominated Pentecostal movements of America and Britain.

However, Black Pentecostalism – particularly Oneness or Apostolic Pentecostalism – has retained more of the 'original' Pentecostal message and power. As Leonard Lovett has stated, black Pentecostalism affirms that,

> ... authentic liberation can never occur apart from genuine pentecostal encounter (i.e. the presence of the Spirit) and likewise, authentic pentecostal encounter does not occur without liberation. No man can genuinely experience the fullness of the Spirit and remain a bona fide racist.[40]

It is among black Pentecostals that we continue to perceive something of Seymour's original emphasis on the liberating, equalising and unifying power of the Spirit.

SEGREGATED CHILDHOOD

Just as infants are unconscious of racial and colour distinctions until those who are 'older and wiser' infect them with prejudice in their childhood, so also the Pentecostal movement enjoyed several years of racial harmony until the divisions on the basis of colour, which had split the older denominations in America, led to the segregation of white from black Pentecostals. Synan wrote that:

> As a glaring exception to the social pattern of the nation, and particularly of the South, the interracial pentecostal groups were subject to great social pressure to conform to the pattern of segregation which with the beginning of the twentieth century dominated most aspects of American life ...
>
> Although some Negroes accepted these divisions as normal and inevitable with some even requesting them, the majority felt that they were 'sinful and embarrassing'. In many cases the

divisions were blamed on the racial 'customs' and 'prejudices' of the South, but never on the prejudices of the whites.[41]

This situation has not improved with the passing of time. Synan admits that:

> In spite of the phenomenal growth of the negro branches of the movement, little recognition of this record has been acknowledged by the white churches. Little or no contact has been maintained between these groups since the interracial period which began in 1906 and ended in 1924. When the 'Pentecostal Fellowship of North America' was formed in 1948 at Des Moines, Iowa, to "demonstrate to the world the essential unity of Spirit-baptized believers, fulfilling the prayers of the Lord Jesus 'that they all may be one'..." not a single Negro denomination was invited to join. Beginning with eight denominations in 1948, the Pentecostal Fellowship of North America added other groups until in 1965 it numbered seventeen denominations – all white.[42]

Leonard Lovett is even more perceptive in his understanding of the causes of racial division. He writes:

> When whites could not 'Europeanise' pentecostalism (Parham led the way by speaking in derogatory terms of certain excesses at the Azusa meeting) and purge it of its 'Africanisms', they separated and formed their own denominations. Thus white pentecostals conceded to the pressure of a racist society.[43]

The Pentecostal movement conformed to the prevailing racist attitudes of white America. White Pentecostals valued and retained glossolalia but neglected or rejected the equality and unity which the Spirit brought to Azusa Street.

The majority of white Pentecostals have ignored, disparaged or sought to discredit the crucial role of Seymour and of black Christians in bringing the Pentecostal movement to birth. However, as Synan correctly recognises: 'Directly or indirectly, practically all of the Pentecostal groups in existence can trace their lineage to the Azusa Mission.'[44] Yet white Pentecostals have generally attempted to obscure or deny the roots of their movement. Parham's sister-in-law even stressed explicitly that 'there were only white persons present at the first Pentecostal shower'. And even blatantly asserted that 'no colored people were ever at the [Texas Bible] school'.[45] Black bishop Seymour, segregated and compelled to listen outside the door, is not even recognised! Nelson states: 'The six best known and most widely quoted primary sources for information on Seymour, written between 1906 and 1939, include five by whites. Two of these go beyond patronising or neglect to noticeable hostility.'[46] Similarly, Lovett notes:

> Previous studies on pentecostalism have not viewed black pentecostalism in its proper historical context because of a failure to appreciate the full spectrum of the heritage of blacks who were numbered among the pentecostals. ... A study of several classical pentecostal writers on the issue of the founding of the contemporary pentecostal movement reveals for the most part a denominational bias and an apparent ommission of the role of blacks. ... It is unfortunate that the blatant omission of Seymour by some classical pentecostal historians is so obvious and becomes a form of judgement on our own ethnic and racial pride.[47]

Many white Pentecostals I have spoken to – both British and American – are profoundly embarrassed by the black origins of their movement and are quick to refute the leading role played by Seymour. They would rather rehabilitate Parham – even if he was homosexual, at least he was white – or deny the existence of human leadership, than accept a black man as their founder.

8 The Spirit and the Wall

... the enslavement of blacks was justified in the name of Christianity. Blacks were made to feel cursed in the name of Christianity. Blacks were excluded from white churches in the name of Christianity. Blacks were [and are] excluded from the benefits of American life in the name of a Christianity which blesses the status quo.

... genuine Christianity affirms a positive black self-concept and actively cooperates with blacks as they struggle to liberate themselves from white oppression.

Columbus Salley and Ronald Behm

In spite of the evangelical fundamentalistic overlay which black Pentecostals owe to their white co-religionists, the leitmotive which sustained black people through the dark night of bondage re-emerged in early Pentecostalism as they had in the Christianity of Negro slaves in the New World.

THE SPIRIT

The spirit possession of West African primal folk religion to some extent paralleled the baptism of the Holy Spirit which brought the presence and power of the divine into the concrete realities of everyday life. The sacred and the profane which were totally integrated in the holistic world view of West Africa were also integrated in black Pentecostalism. God was experienced in all of life, bringing power, liberty, joy and solace. Black people perceived Him as with them in the diaspora, in slavery, and in the racist culture of the United States. They believed that the same Spirit which had been in Christ and in the Apostles was in them as they carried salvation and healing to the urban ghettos of America. Not only did the Spirit equip them to transform society – to obliterate the colour line through the power of love – She also liberated them spiritually, psychologically and socially, transforming poor, dispossessed, disenfranchised, ill-educated, powerless black people who were despised and constantly being told that they were inferior by white society. Their self concept was changed, for now they were the children of god – the Saints of the Most High! Their pneumatic experience affirmed black dignity and lifted the believer out of the mundane into 'ecstatic' consciousness of God's presence, power and love. The black Pentecostal, like the African, used music and rhythm as a means of attuning himself to the Spirit – as a vehicle for the power of God. Thus possessed by the Spirit, the black Pentecostal sang and danced in the celebration of life in the same way as his parents and grandparents had done during slavery, and in ways his ancestors would have recognised in West Africa.

To say that the spirit possession of Africa and the Holy Spirit baptism of Pentecostalism are phenomenologically similar, raises the question: Was the Holy Spirit in Africa before the gospel was carried there, and could the spirit which possessed their forefathers in Africa be the same as that which baptises black Pentecostals today? If we accept the 'filioque' pneumatology of the Western churches – including Western Pentecostals and Charismatics – then the answer must be no. To understand the Holy Spirit as proceeding 'from the Father and the Son' is, in effect, to insist that the Christian Church has a monopoly on the Spirit of God. However, such a view tends to negate the doctrine of the Holy Spirit as it appears in the Old Testament. For the early Hebrew writers, the Ruach Yahweh was not only the Spirit which possessed the 'Judges' and 'men of God', She was also the source of *all* life. Because the Eastern churches – Old Catholic and Orthodox – understand the Spirit as proceeding from the Father alone, they are open to the pneumatology of the Old Testament and are thus more able to appreciate that the Spirit of God is the Spirit of all life – the creator and sustainer; the vital force.[1] Thus, the pneumatology of the East is open to the idea of the presence of the Ruach Yahweh in Africa before the arrival of the gospel, and perhaps even to pre-Christian possession by the Holy Spirit which is analogous to that of the Old Testament.[2]

In spite of phenomenological similarities however, the cognitive differences are acute. Western Pentecostals have adopted a predominantly Lucan pneumatology and emphasise the positive moral and ethical influence of (or prerequisites for receiving) the Holy Spirit, within an almost exclusively Christocentric view. In stark contrast to this is the amoral concept of spiritual power found in West African primal religion. The One Spirit of

Western theology is also very different from the plurality of spirits in African belief. But in spite of these cognitive differences, there is much in the pneumatologies of the Old Testament and of Paul which contradict the Western (and Western Pentecostal) understanding of the Spirit and suggest some commonality with the pneumatology of West African primal religions. For example, Paul's letter to the Corinthian church emphasises that there can be a sharp disjunction between the power of the Spirit and morality.[3] The Old Testament speaks of evil and lying spirits sent to men by God,[4] and the Apocalypse, albeit figuratively, refers to 'the spirits of God'.[5]

Although black Pentecostals in the Americas and Britain generally express the same pneumatology as their white counterparts, there are occasional hints of an amoral understanding of spiritual power[6] and, while white Pentecostals stress possessing the Spirit, black Pentecostals are more concerned to be possessed by the Spirit. 'Let all things be done decently and in order' and 'the spirits of the prophets are subject to the prophets', stressed by white Pentecostalism, contrast to some extent with the exhortations of black Pentecostals to 'let the Spirit have His way' and 'quench not the Spirit'.[7]

In spite of an overt and superficial conformity to the narrow white Pentecostal definition of charismata, black Pentecostals – in practice if not always in theory – perceive the Spirit as working through them in the gifts of story and song, testimony and prayer, vision and dream, dance and motor behaviour, shouting and the drama of the sermon – all manifestations of the power and love of God. For white Pentecostals, the charismata were soon restricted to the nine referred to in 1 Corinthians 12, and even they were understood in the narrowest and most limited sense. Tongues and physical healing were exalted, but they rejected the power and love which transcended race and colour, could create the interracial community of God's people and could bring healing for the hurts caused by the social diseases of slavery and racism.

THE CHURCH

For early black-inspired Pentecostalism, the Church was not an organisation but the community of God's people – the family of

God. It was composed of those who were – there and then – the children of God. Those who would one day (and that day was near at hand) rejoice with Jesus in the Kingdom of God. Furthermore, they were the agents of the revolution about to break on the world with the Second Advent of Christ. They were God's ambassadors bringing the Kingdom near as they lived out the Bible in twentieth-century America. To bring life and salvation and healing and reconciliation and hope was their mission to the world. Love was more than an abstract concept or verbal affirmation, it was a living, tangible, practical reality.

Early Pentecostal (and a great deal of contemporary black Pentecostal) worship was holistic and all-embracing – heart and mind and body and emotions were given over to the celebration of life and hope. Worship was social and communal, not individualistic and private. It built up the Christian community and incorporated the individual into the family of God. All were able to participate in the worshipping community through music and singing, rhythmic motion and antiphonal responses, testifying and simultaneous praying, governing and leading, even cooking and cleaning. No one was a spectator; all were actors. No one was excluded on the grounds of illiteracy or lack of ability, for what was done was not done primarily for man to glory in or for people to be entertained by. It was done for God and it sprang, not from the intellect but from the heart. To sing or testify or pray was a liberating experience. Neither the words nor the music were to be judged but rather the sincerity of the speaker or singer. For many white Pentecostals these activities soon became threatening rather than liberating. The illiterate, inarticulate or unmelodious fell silent for fear that their performance was deficient. The community was once again reduced to an audience.

Black Pentecostalism has also changed for the worse as divisions caused by struggles for dominance and status have been rationalised in terms of spurious doctrinal differences.

The black Pentecostal worshipping community had – and still has – tremendous integrative power. Past, present and future; the seen and unseen world; God and man; man and his fellow man; all could be drawn together. It is a phenomenon which is difficult to describe to those who have never partici-pated (rather than spectated) in black Pentecostal worship. The rhythms, music, heterophonus singing, responses and simultaneous praying combine together in a gestalt – the total is more than, and indeed transcends the sum of the parts. The Spirit moves in the corporate worship and God is immanent. The music and singing and shouting liberates and opens up the worshipper to the power of the divine.

THE WALL

White Pentecostals, with few exceptions, tore asunder the interracial worshipping community of equals, and in their struggles for dominance and conformity to particular fundamentalistic interpretations of the Bible, they destroyed Seymour's dream on the altar of racial supremacy. Black Pentecostals, like their forefathers in slavery, witnessed once again the hypocrisy of white Christians, yet clung to the faith which they had received from them – a faith underpinned by the black leitmotive yet still substantially inherited from white Americans. One of the miracles of history is that so many black people have, in spite of everything, remained steadfast Christians.

With the redrawing of the colour line by the white Pentecostals, the black worshipping community became an ethnic community, as it had been in Africa and during slavery. There the black person in a racist society, could have his humanity and dignity affirmed. There he could find an outlet for the self expression, creativity and diverse abilities which were stifled by white society. Self determination and leadership could develop in an environment which was not disadvantageous to those who had limited education and a black culture as well as a black skin. Oral liturgy and narrative theology – the heritage of West Africa and slavery – were not overwhelmed by the literary or systematic methods of Western Christianity.

While white Pentecostalism tended to revert to type and increasingly conformed to Western, middle class evangelical tradition, on the other side of the wall black Pentecostalism, with its African spirituality, hand clapping, antiphonal singing and motor behaviour reaffirmed the black leitmotive which had survived the Middle Passage, sustained black Christians during slavery and continues to give them dignity, power and hope in a society which has had its prejudice mirrored by the white churches and its racism justified by a heretical Christianity.

Notes and References

FOREWORD

1. Lovett, Leonard, 'Black Origins of the Pentecostal Movement' in Synan, Vinson (ed.), *Aspects of Pentecostal–Charismatic Origins* (Plainfield, New Jersey: Logos International, 1975) p. 138; Lovett, Leonard, 'Perspective on the Black Origins of the Contemporary Pentecostal Movement', in *The Journal of the Interdenominational Theological Center*, vol. 1 (Atlanta, Georgia 1973) pp 42–6. Quoted by MacRobert, pp. 9 and 77f.
2. Nelson, Douglas J., *For Such a Time as This: the Story of Bishop William J. Seymour and the Azusa Street Revival*, unpublished Ph.D. dissertation, University of Birmingham, May 1981, pp. 31, 153–8. Quoted by MacRobert, p. 35.
3. *The Apostolic Faith*, Los Angeles, vol. I, no. 1, Sept. 1906, p. 1, col. 1. Quoted by MacRobert, p. 55.
4. Synan, Vinson, *The Holiness–Pentecostal Movement in The United States*, (Grand Rapids, Michigan: William B. Eerdmans Publishing Co., 1971) p. 168. Quoted by MacRobert, p. 83, see also p. 82.
5. MacRobert, p. 2.
6. *1 Cor. 14:4:* ὁ λαλῶν γλώσσῃ ἑαυτὸν οἰκοδομεῖ.

INTRODUCTION

1. Van Dusen, Henry Pitt, 'The Third Force in Christendom' in *Life*, 9 June 1958, p. 13. The 'Third Force in Christendom' includes, according to van Dusen, The Churches of Christ, The Seventh Day of Adventists, Nazarenes, Jehovah's Witnesses, and the Christian and Missionary Alliance, but 'the largest single group is the 8.5 million Pentecostals', Ibid., p. 124.
2. Van Dusen, Henry Pitt, 'Caribbean Holiday' in *Christian Century*, 17 Aug. 1955, p. 948; Van Dusen, Henry Pitt, 'Montana Indians and Pentecostals', in *Christian Century*, 23 July 1958, p. 850.
3. Hollenweger, Walter J., *The Pentecostals* (London: SCM Press, 1972) pp. XVII, XVIII.
4. Barrett, David B., 'AD 2000: 350 Million Christians in Africa' in *International Review of Mission*, vol. 59, no. 233, Jan. 1970, pp. 39–54; Barrett, David B. (ed.), *World Christian Encyclopedia* (Oxford University Press, 1982).

   By 'Pentecostal type' I am referring to those Christian sects and denominations which conform to the 'black roots' pattern summarised by Hollenweger and quoted in the introduction.

Pentecostalism is also becoming less identified with the poor and ill-educated as the neo-Pentecostal or Charismatic movement within the mainstream denominations has gained acceptance and respectability. In 1975, more than ten thousand Pentecostal Catholics gathered at St. Peter's in Rome to receive the endorsement of Pope Paul VI. And in 1978 some two thousand Pentecostal Anglicans met in Canterbury Cathedral to be addressed by Archbishop Donald Coggin. Synan, Vinson, in the foreword to Bartleman, Frank, *Azusa Street* (Plainfield NJ: Logos International, 1980) p. XXIV.

5. Williams, Cyril G., *Tongues of the Spirit* (Cardiff: University of Wales Press, 1981) p. 38.

6. Studies of black Pentecostalism in Britain have tended to be of limited value because they have ignored the influences Africa and of slavery upon black Christianity. Hill (1963, 1971) and Calley (1965) ignore them completely. Root (1979) only touches on them, and Price (1979) while including an excellent chapter on 'Social and Cultural Origins', has only as limited understanding of Pentecostalism: Hill, Clifford, *West Indian Migrants and the London Churches* (Oxford University Press, for IRR, 1963); Hill, Clifford, *Black Churches: West Indian Sects in Britain*, Community and Race Relations Unit of the Britain Council of Churches, 1971; Calley, Malcolm, *God's People* (Oxford University Press, 1965); Root, John, *Encountering West Indian Pentecostalism: Its Ministry and Worship* (Bramcote, Notts: Grove Books, 1979); Pryce, Ken, *Endless Pressure: a Study of West Indian Life-Styles in Bristol* (Middx: Penguin Books, 1979).

7. Hollenweger, Walter J., 'After Twenty Years' Research on Pentecostalism' in *Theology*, vol. LXXXVII, no. 720, Nov. 1982, pp. 405–6.

CHAPTER 1: SOME GLOSSOLALIC PRECURSORS

1. *The Apostolic Faith*, vol. 1, no. 1, Sept. 1906, p. 2, col. 1.

2. 'Fundamental Beliefs of the Elim Pentecostal Church' in *Elim Evangel*.

3. Barratt, T. B., *Urkristendommen*, p. 14 quoted in Bloch-Hoell, Nils, *The Pentecostal Movement*, (Oslo: Universitetsforlaget; London: Allen & Unwin, 1964) p. 1. Explicit Biblical references to glossolalia are to be found in Acts 2:4, 33; 10:46; 19:6; 1 Corinthians 12:10; 12:30; 13:1,8; 14:1–39 and Mark 16:17. However, the final paragraphs of this chapter are omitted from Codex Vaticanus and Codex Sinaiticus and are considered to be a later addition. Concerning this passage, Kelsey writes: 'Although it may be doubtful that these were the direct words of Jesus, this passage certainly represents the experience and expectation of the early Church. In fact, the very probability that it comes from the second century makes it all the more significant. It then becomes a primary indication that the practise of tongues was not confined to the first days of the Church' (Kelsey, Morton, T., *Tongues Speaking: an Experiment in Spiritual Experience* [London: Hodder and Stoughton, 1968] p. 25).
    Other possible allusions to glossolalia are found in Acts 8:14–25;

4:23–32; 1 Thess. 5:19,20; Col. 3:16; Eph. 5:18–20; James 3:1–8; Gal. 4:6; Romans 8:14, 15, 26, 27; John 3:8.

4. Gee, Donald, *The Pentecostal Movement* (London: Elim Publishing Co., 1949) pp. 7–8.

5. 'The Declaration of Faith of the Church of God (Cleveland)' printed on the cover of *Church of God Egangel*.

6. Anderson, Robert M., *A Social History of the Early Twentieth Century Pentecostal Movement*, Columbia University, Ph.D. Thesis 1969 (*High Wycombe*: University Microfilms, High Wycombe, 1972) pp. 10–11. Published in a revised form as *Vision of the Disinherited: the Making of American Pentecostalism*, (New York: Oxford University Press, 1979).

7. Kelsey suggests that the apostolic fathers probably included references to the phenomenon of glossolalia by alluding to it as prophecy. He also proposes that the virtual silence of the Church fathers conerning glossolalia may have been due to their fear of adding 'fuel to the fire that flamed into irrational rejection of Christians as monsters or, at best, queer people' rather than to the cessation of tongues. Kelsey. pp. 3–7. Cyril G. Williams believes that the New Testament and twentieth century Pentecostal phenomena of glossolalia are related of the psychological conditions under which prophecy was forthcoming in the Old Testament. He writes:

> I am not arguing for a lineal development from early Hebrew prophetic conditions to modern day glossolalia experience. In fact ... there is no evidence of glossolalia per se in the Old Testament, but nevertheless may psychological features associated with the glossolal-ist experience are present, as well as similarities in the conception of the role of the Spirit. What I am urging is due recognition for the respectable role of the non-rational in religiou experience, a factor which is more readily evident in ecstaticism than in normal religious behaviour. I contend in fact, that varying degrees of ecstatic dissociation are present in Hebrew prophecy and that the psychologi-cal conditions may parallel the variety of states encountered in modern glossolalic behaviour, making a distinction of course, between the state or condition and the utterance which derives from it.
> Williams, Cyril, G., *Tongues of the Spirit* (Cardiff: University of Wales Press, 19–1) p. 11 *passim*

I use the term 'ecstatic' in its broadest sense to refer to any behaviour which involves the breaking through of the unconscious into conscious-ness. This can range from states of total dissociation or frenzy to the relaxed and controlled use of glossolalia in states of heightened awareness, consciousness, sensitivity and perceptivity.

8. Bruner, Frederick, Dale, *A Theology of the Holy Spirit* (London: Hodder & Stoughton, 1970) p. 36.

9. Ibid., p. 36. Whether or not the Montanists spoke in tongues is debatable. Cutten, George Barton, *Speaking with Tongues: Historically and Psychologically Considered* (New Haven: Yale University Press, 1927) p. 35; Currie, S. D., 'Speaking in Tongues: Early Evidence Outside the New Testament Bearing on Glossais Lalein' in *Interpretation*, 19 July

1965, p. 288. However, it would appear that the ability to speak in tongues was possessed by Montanus himself and his two associates, the Prophetesses Priscilla and Maximilla. Lietzmann, Hans, *The Founding of the Church Universal* (New York: Meridin Books, 1963, pp. 54–61, 194–202; Knox, Ronald A., *Enthusiasm: a Chapter in Religion with Special Reference to the 17th and 18th Centuries*, (New York: Oxford University Press, 1961) pp. 25–49.

10. Seeberg, Reinhold, *Text-Book of the History of Doctrines*, trans. Hay, Charles E. (Grand Rapids, Michigan: Baker Book House, 1956) pp. 105–6 , quoted in Bruner, op. cit., p. 36.

11. Cf. Hollenweger, *The Pentecostals* (London: SCM Press, 1972) pp. 311–12.

12. The Egyptian Abbot, St. Pachomius, who lived in the 4th century may have practised glossolalia, and the Greek and Orthodox Church in the East developed a tradition in which, according to Kelsey, the gifts of the Spirit, including glossolalia, continued without attracting particular attention (Kelsey, pp. 7, 38, 41–6).

13. Anderson, p. 23; Knox, pp. 356–65, 372–88; Kelsey, pp. 52–5.
     There is also evidence for pre-Christian glossolalia. See, Anderson, pp. 15, 16 and Gromacki, Robert, G., *The Modern Tongues Movement* (Phillipsburg, N.J. Presbyterian and Reformed Publishing Company, 1967) pp. 5–8.

14. Anderson, p. 24; Knox, pp. 365–71.

15. Anderson, p. 25; Andrews, Edward, D., *The People Called Shakers: a Search for the Perfect Society* (New York: Oxford University Press, 1953) pp. 144–6, 153–4, 237–8; Cross, Whitney R. *The Burned Over District* (New York: Harper & Row, 1965) pp. 31–3, 310–11.

16. Anderson, p. 27; Shaw, E., *The Catholic Apostolic Church* (New York: King's Crown Press, 1946); Drummond, Andrew L., *Edward Irving and His Circle* (London: James Clark and Co., 1935); Strachan, Gordon, *The Pentecostal Theology of Edward Irving* (London: Darton, Longmann & Todd, 1973); Christenson, Larry, 'Pentecostalism's Forgotten Forerunner' in Synan, Vinson (ed.), *Aspects of Pentecostal-Charasmatic Origins* (Plainfield, New Jersey: Logos International, 1975) pp. 15–37; Kelsey, pp. 58–9; O'Dea, Thomas, F., *The Mormons* (University of Chicago Press, 1957) pp. 158–60; Synan, Vinson, *The Holiness-Pentecostal Movement in the United States* (Grand Rapids, Michigan: William B. Eerdmans Publishing Co., 1961) pp. 25–6.
     The Spiritualist Movement also came into being at this time (1848) with the rappings heard by the Fox sisters near Rochester, New York. Sceances included carrying out a variety of acts such as writing, singing, playing musical instruments, speaking intelligibly and speaking in tongues under the control of spirits.

17. Anderson, p. 27; Loud, Grover, C., *Evangelised America* (New York: Dial Press, 1928, p. 176).

18. Anderson, pp. 27, 26.

19. Nickel, Thomas, R., *The Amazing Shakarian Story* (Los Angeles: Full Gospel Business Men's Fellowship International, 1964) *passim*. The nineteenth-century glossolalic sect, the Molokans, were responsible for

introducing the Shakarin family to glossolalia. Samarin, W. J., *Tongues of Men and Angels* (Toronto: Collier MacMillan, 1972) pp. 130, 184; Anderson, p. 107; Kelsey, pp. 59, 65–8.

20. Synan, *Holiness–Pentecostal*, p. 114.
21. Lovett, Leonard, 'Black Origins of the Pentecostal Movement' in Synan, *Aspects*, p. 138.

BLACK AMERICAN CHRISTIANITY

1. Frazier, E. Franklin, *The Negro Church in America* (New York: Schocken Books, 1974 (originally 1964) pp. 9–13; cf. Dorson, Richard M., *American Folk Lore* (University of Chicago Press, 1959) *passim*. Dorson argues for a predominantly European origin for the folk lore of black people in the Southern States, and a predominantly African origin for that of the Caribbean and South America. A view which is not entirely shared by the author.

2. Frazier, p. 16. Frazier also sees the adoption of Christianity by slaves as a means of obtaining some temporary solidarity and union with their fellow men, including the white slave masters. However, a more credible analysis is given by Herskovits, Wilmore, Washington and Raboteau who, while stressing the sense of community associated with black Christianity, also make it clear that it was to some extent a radical protest against the conditions and perpetrators of slavery. Herskovits, Melville J., *The Myth of the Negro Past* (Boston: Beacon Press, 1958). For a summary of Herskovits' research and the debate between Herskovits and Frazier see Raboteau, op. cit., pp. 48–55. Herskovits maintains that Negro slaves developed a 'principle of disregard' for the outer forms of religious practice but retained its 'inner values', pp. 296–8: Wilmore, Gayroud S., *Black Religion and Black Radicalism* (New York: Doubleday and Co., 1972; Cone, James H., *The Spirituals and the Blues: an Interpretation* (New York: The Seabury Press, 1972); Washington, Joseph R., *Black Sects and Cults* (Garden City, New York: Anchor Press/Doubleday, 1973); Raboteau, Albert J., *Slave Religion: the Invisible Institution in the Antebellum South* (Oxford University Press, 1978). see also Savannah Unit, Georgia Writers' Project, *Drums and Shadows* (University of Georgia Press) 1960, and Bastide, Roger, *African Civilisations in the New World*, trans. Peter Green) (London: Ch. Hurst & Co., 1971) (originally Les Ameriques Noirs, Paris: Editions Payot, 1967).

3. Wilmore, pp. 1–5.
Christianity was established in North Africa at a very early date and, as Mommsen has so eloquently stated:

> It was through Africa that Christianity became the religion of the world. Tertullian and Cyprian were from Charthage, Arnobius from Sicca, Veneria, Lactantius, and probably in like manner Minucius Felix, in-spite of their Latin names, were natives of Africa, and not

less so Augustin. In Africa the Church found its most zealous
confessors of the faith and its most gifted defenders.

Quoted in DuBois, W. E. Burghardt, *The Negro* (London: Oxford
University Press, 1970; originally 1915) p. 77

3. The Church was also established in East Africa from the Nile Delta to
    the Gulf of Aden. The ancient Church of Africa still survives in
    Ethiopia. However it was not from West Africa that most of the slaves
    were brought to the New World. In the sixteenth Century the
    Portuguese had some success in spreading Catholicism among the
    inhabitants of both East and West coasts.
4. Wilmore, ibid., pp. 1–5.
5. Ibid., p. 18.
6. Raboteau, pp. 4–5.
7. Cone, pp. 29–30. See also the Preacher Tales in which the Christian
    minister is severely criticised for hypocrisy. Dorson, Richard M.,
    American Negro Folktales (Greenwich, Connecticut: Fawcett Publications,
    1967) p. 254.
8. Washington, p. 20.
9. Ibid., pp. 24–6, 31. Williams, Joseph J., *Psychic Phenomena of Jamaica*
    (Westport, Conn.: Greenwood Press (originally New York: Dial Press),
    1979 (originally 1934) pp. 69–70; Bascom, William, 'Folklore and
    Literature' in Lystad, Robert A. (ed.), *The African World: a Survey of
    Social Research* (London: Pall Mall Press for African Studies Association,
    1965; pp. 468–73, 475, 478–86.

    Under slavery, children were usually separated from their parents to
    be brought up by the old women who were no longer capable of field
    labour. This section of the slave population, because of age, were most
    likely to dwell on the past and thus pass on the lore and values of
    African society; Bastide, p. 89; Mbiti, john S. *African Religions and
    Philosophy* (London: Heineman 1969) p. 67.

    Excellent collections of oral 'scriptures' have been made by Gaba,
    Christian R. *Scriptures of an African People: Ritual Utterances of the Anlo*
    (New York: Nok Publishers, 1973) and Bascom, William, *Ifa Divination:
    Communication Between Gods and Men in West Africa* (Indiana University
    Press, 1969) pp. 120–563.

    See also Beier, Ulli, *The Return of the Gods: the Sacred Art of Susanne
    Wegner* (Cambridge University Press) 1975.
10. Washington, p. 20; Gaba, pp. 1–3; Mbiti, John S., *Introduction to African
    Religion* (London: Heineman, 1975) pp. 22–7, 102 *passim*.

    I use the term 'folk' religion because the indigenous religions of Africa
    belong to the people. They are 'indigenous' in that they are not only
    native to Africa, but as far as we are aware, also originated there. The
    term 'primal' is not used in the sense of 'primitive' but rather to express
    the idea of being 'original' or 'first in time'. African religion may also be
    described as 'traditional' – that is transmitted orally from generation to
    generation. John V. Taylor, who coined the word 'primal' with reference
    to indigenous African religion, most commonly refers to it as 'traditional
    religion' as does Idowu: Taylor, John V., *The Primal Vision: Christian*

Presence Amid African Religion (London: SCM Press, 1963) pp. 18–20 *passim*; see also pp. 85–108; Idowu, E. Bolaji, *African Traditional Religion: a Definition* (London: SCM Press, 1973) pp. 103–4; Mbiti, *Philosophy*, pp. 2, 4, 15–16.

For a consideration of other terms used to describe indigenous African religion see Idowu, pp. 108–36.

The idea expressed by the Zulu: 'nmuntu ngumuntu ngabantu' – a person is only a human being in relation to other people – is a concept common throughout Africa. J. H. Oldham expressed it thus: 'the isolated individual is an abstraction. We become persons only in and through our relations with other persons. The individual self has no independent existence which gives it the power to enter into relationships with other selves. Only through intercourse with other selves can it become a self at all' (Oldham, J. H. in *The Times*, 5 Oct. 1933, quoted in Taylor, p. 57).

11. Wilmore, pp. 19–20.

12. Similar or related views of reality are to be found in Hebraic thought. The Star of David illustrates the intermeshing of the two triangles of the natural and spiritual worlds. In pre-enlightenment Europe and in some rural areas of Britain today such beliefs are discernible, as they are in the later writings of Carl C. Jung and of Arthur Koestler. In fact Koestler's 'party trick' of causing two paper clips – each representing a different aspect of reality – to link by placing them on a bank note is analogous to the interrelationship illustrated by the two triangles of the Jewish Star. A similar interrelationship between the natural and spiritual world was propounded by Emmanual Swedenborg (1688 to 1772) and his New Jerusalem Church. Swedenborg also held to a modalistic view of the Godhead similar to that of the Oneness Pentecostals. See also Taylor, pp. 146–63, 189.

13. Wilmore, pp. 8, 20–5; Raboteau, pp. 7–16, 33–4, 275–88; Washington, pp. 28–9; DuBois, *The Negro* pp. 74–7; Williams, pp. 59–60, 63, 65–8; Parrinder, Geoffrey, 'The African Spiritual Universe' in Gates, Brian, *Afro-Caribbean Religions* (London: Ward Lock Educational, 1980) p. 19; Metuh, Emefie Ikenga, *God and Man in African Religion* (London: Geoffrey Chapman/Cassell Ltd., 1981) p. 54 *passim*; Awolalu, J. Omosade, *Yoruba Beliefs and Sacrificial Rites* (London: Longman, 1979) *passim*; Bascom, pp. 3–119 *passim*; Taylor, pp. 59–76, cf. p. 80; Epega, Daniel Olarimwa, *The Basis of Yoruba Religion* (Nigeria: Ijamido Printers, 1971) *passim*; Mbiti, *Introduction*, pp. 12, 32–5, 44–53 *passim*; Mbiti *Philosophy*, pp. 25–7, 29–49, 58–76, 75–91, 150–6, 158–61, 163–81, 187–203; Mbiti, John S., *Concepts of God in Africa* (London: SPCK, 1969) *passim*; Idowu, pp. 137–202. see also Braithwaite, Edward Kamau, *The Folk Culture of the Slaves in Jamaica* (London: New Beacon Books, 1981) pp. 11–12 *passim*; Gaba, pp. 1–4 *passim*.

The term 'diffused monotheism' was coined by Idowu, op. cit., pp. 135–136; see also Taylor, pp. 59, 77–145.

The significance of sacrifice in Ikbo (Ibo) religion has been dealt with by Arinze, Francis A., *Sacrifice in Ibo Religion* (Ibadan, Nigeria: Ibadan University Press, 1970). Africans of the diaspora had a holistic world view which integrated man with the supernatural, his fellow man, his dead ancestors and the animal kingdom.

In Africa the Supreme Being was rarely if ever represented by statues or carvings.

Because the theology and liturgy of traditional African folk religion is oral, there are no ancient written records from which we can learn what that religion was like before and during the early days of slavery. The earliest accounts by Europeans are unreliable so that we must rely on modern studies of current African belief and practise. Some of these – particularly as they relate to West Africa – are summarised in Parrinder, pp. 17–18.

14. Raboteau, pp. 11–12.
15. Washington, pp. 20–1, 29. Washington argues that the 'essence' of all black religion, of whatever persuasion, is the 'ethnic ethic' of the community which seeks for the power of the spirit 'as the way to the secular power rather than as a substitute for it'. 'Any sectarian movement', writes Washington, 'which focuses on a priority other than gaining real power in this real world runs counter to the central black religious intention. Ecstasy, tradition, and enthusiasm contribute to keeping blacks attune to the fullness of life and power, and where they serve to interest blacks in sheerly intangible things we have the impact of white domination.' pp. xi, 1. See also Mbiti, *Philosophy*, pp. 182–3 and Beckman, David M., 'Black Indigenous Churches' in *Afro-American Studies*, no. 3, 1975, pp. 251–2.
16. Wilmore, pp. 1, 14; Washington, p. 30.
17. Wilmore, pp. 15–17; Mbiti, *Introduction*, pp. 156, 201.
18. Raboteau, p. 15.
19. Ibid., pp. 35–6; Williams, pp. 69–70; see also Taylor, p. 77.
20. DuBois, W. E. Burghart, *The Negro Church* (Atlanta University Press, 1903) p. 5; Wilmore, pp. 27–9; Raboteau, pp. 9–10; Haskins, James, *Witchcraft, Mysticism and Magic in the Black World*, (Garden City, New York: Doubleday and Co. Inc., 1974) pp. 13f.

The word 'tribe' is used, not to suggest some negative evaluation but simply with reference to different ethno-linguistic groups or clans. Williams, p. 61.

Many Africans today reject elements of Western culture as did Africans of the diaspora. John V. Taylor points out that these rejections 'focus mainly on the European concept of individualism, upon the supremacy of the cerebral over the sensuous and intuitive, and upon the attitude of domination towards nature' (Taylor, p. 24).

21. Jones, Charles Colcock, *The Religious Instruction of Negroes in the United States*, (Savannah: T. Porse Co., 1842) pp. 125f, quoted in Wilmore, p. 10.
22. Wilmore, pp. 21–2. For a summary of early and more recent studies of African primal religion by Europeans, see Mbiti, *Philosophy*, pp. 6–14. Terms such as 'animism' and 'fetishism' were not coined until much later, but the ideas they express were current among Christian missions to slaves. See also Idowu, pp. 120–34. The European inability to understand the world of the African is partly due to his tendency to internalise his fears and desires while the African externalises them.

Taylor touched on this when he noted that '. . . the European represses the things in himself that he is afraid of, the African projects them. The European is on guard against the self he has battoned down in his own mind; the African is on guard against the self he has externalised into the world around', Taylor, p. 168. For the European, the id, the superego and all of his represessed memories and desires are perceived as within the individual subconscious mind. For the African, the id is in the world around him – both natural and supernatural; the superego is the community – family and tribe, both present and past (sin is not so much personal unrighteousness as anti-social activity); and memories of the past are carried into the present and concretised in people, artifacts and nature.

23. Raboteau, p. 103; DuBois, *The Negro*, p. 112; Washington, Booker, T., and DuBois, W. E. Burghardt, *The Negro in the South* (New York: The Citadel Press, 1970, originally the Wiliam Levi Bull Lectures for 1907, pp. 127–8. See also pp. 129–31; Hamilton, Charles, V., *The Black Preacher in America* (New York: William Morrow and Co., 1972) pp. 37–69. For a comprehensive synopsis of early black Christian leaders see Washington and DuBois, pp. 141–52.

In 1667 Virginia followed other states and legislated that conversion to Christianity had no bearing on slavery: 'Baptism doth not alter the condition of the person as to his bondage or freedom, in order that diverse masters freed from this doubt may more carefully endevor the propagation of Christianity,' quoted in DuBois, *The Negro*, p. 112.

24. Wilmore, pp. 7–9; Raboteau, pp. 6–7; Frazier, pp. 14, 29–31.

The Baptists were foremost in licensing black preachers at the end of the eighteenth century. For a fuller account of the religious instruction of slaves and of the first black ordinands, see Raboteau, pp. 97–150, 134–5.

25. Redkey, Edwin S., *Black Exodus*, (Newhaven: Yale University Press, 1969), pp. 30f, quoted in Wilmore, p. 34. See also numerous examples in Yetman, Norman, R., *Voices from Slavery* (New York: Holt, Reinhart & Winston, 1970).

26. Wilmore, pp. 41–4. For an account of anti-slavery views among some seventeenth century Quakers see Raboteau, p. 111.

27. Wilmore, pp. 33–4; Arinze, pp. 34–6; Awolalu, pp. 158–9.

The world view of Africa and the Hebraic world view have much in common with each other and little in common with that of Europe.

Orisha is a Yoruba word for a lesser deity while Olorun is the name of the Supreme Being. See also Bastide, pp. 115–22.

28. Mbiti, *Philosophy*, pp. 58–66, 92–9, 149–65 *passim*; Mbiti, *Introduction*, pp. 55–60, 77–9, 80–1, 110–111, 116–22 *passim*; Taylor, pp. 73, 76, 170; Raboteau, pp. 126–7; Washington, p. 32; Williams, p. 61. Belief in rewards or punishments in the hereafter is uncommon in Africa generally but is found in Nigeria and Ghana – regions from which many people were taken as slaves to the New World. The Ashanti and many other West Africans also believe in a personal devil.

29. Cone, p. 46. The words of this spiritual in a slightly diffrent form, were quoted by the Negro civil rights leader, Martin Luther King, in his

'Dream' speech: 'Free at last, free at last, thank God Almighty, we are free at last.' And they inspired the words on his gravestone: 'FREE AT LAST, FREE AT LAST, THANK GOD ALMIGHTY, I'M FREE AT LAST.'

30. Wilmore, pp. 5, 15, 18, 31.
31. Cone, pp. 80–1.
32. Wilmore, pp. 11, 13–14, 17, 19, 25–6, 34; Mbiti, *Introduction*, pp. 175–81; Taylor, pp. 172–6ff; Cone, p. 35; Raboteau, pp. 122, 125, 294–7, 299–302, 305–11.
33. Raboteau, pp. 128–36. Examples of religious reciprocacy between black slave and white master are cited in Raboteau, pp. 316, 317. Examples of black ministers serving white congregations are given in Hamilton, pp. 42–3.
34. Raboteau, p. 149.
35. Ibid., pp. 152–9, 171–3.
36. Ibid., pp. 165–7.
37. Ibid., pp. 160–1; Synan, Vinson, *The Holiness–Pentecostal Movement in the United States* (Michigan: William B. Eerdmans Publishing Co., 1971) pp. 30–1.

     H. Richard Neibuhr notes that: 'The attitude of the early Methodists and Baptists towards slavery had been that of men whose own economic and social condition made them sensitive to the sins of inequality and oppression.' With the enbourgeoisement of these groups, and their development from sects into denominations, the congregations in the South modified and ultimately reversed their original opposition to slavery (Neibuhr, Richard H., *The Social Sources of Denominationalism* [New York: Living Age Books, 1957; originally 1929] pp. 191–5).
38. Neibuhr, pp. 191, 195–9.
39. Ibid., pp. 188–9.
40. Wilmore, pp. 48–9, 51–2, 80f; Raboteau, pp. 116–20, 311–13; Cone, pp. 34–8, 45. For a fuller treatment of the subject of slave literacy and the Bible, see Raboteau, pp. 239–43.

     Many of the syncretistic cults of Africa also identify themselves with the Hebrews of the Old Testament. Lanternari, Vittorio, *The Religions of the Oppressed: a Study of Modern Messianic Cults*, trans. Sergio, Lisa (LOndon: MacGibbon & Kee, 1963) p. 62.
41. Aptheker, Herbert, *American Negro Slave Revolts*, (New York: International Publishers, 1978; originally p1943) p. 128.
42. Quoted in Wilmore, p. 133.
43. Quoted in Wilmore, p. 137 and in extracts from Walker, David, 'Walker's Appeal in Four Articles: Together With a Preamble, to the Colored Citizens of the World, but in particular, and very expressly to those in the United States of America', Boston, Massachusetts, 28 Sept. 1829. Quoted in Aptheker, Herbert, *A Documentary History of the Negro People in the United States* (New York: Citadel Press, 1969) p. 96.
44. Wilmore, pp. 61–2, 64, 68, 74–8, 80–3. For an account and analysis of slave insurrections see Aptheker, *Revolts, passim.*
45. DuBois, W. E. Burghardt, *The Souls of Black Folks*, (New York: Aaron Books, 1965) pp. 147–8.

46. Wilmore, pp. 64, 67, 77–8, 82; Frazier, p. 26; Raboteau, pp. 98–9, 123; Caldecott, Alfred, *The Church in the West Indies* (London: Frank Cass, 1970) pp. 65–6, 70; Aptheker, *Documentary History*, p. 120; Aptheker, *Revolts*, p. 59.

   Religion and the desire for freedom had been further linked and confused in the eightenth century when Church and civil courts debated the Portuguese custom of freeing baptised slaves. Consequently, many slaves saw baptism and the adoption of their master's religion as a means of obtaining liberty and perhaps equality.

47. Wilmore, pp. 68–9. For an account of slave insurrections prior to 1800 see Aptheker, *Revolts*, pp. 162–208; see also Mullins, G. W. *Flight and Rebellion: Slave Resistance in Eighteenth Century Virginia* (New York: Oxford University Press, 1972) pp. 140–204 *passim*.

   Concerning the drawing of the colour line through the denominations in the United States, Neibuhr writes:

   > The social causes of schism have been obscured so frequently by theological rationalisation that the frankness with which the color line has been drawn in the church is unusual. No partisan maintains that the Colored Methodist Episcopal Church and the Methodist Episcopal Church, South, were divided from each other by heresy or that the separation of the colored from the white Baptists was occasioned by doctrinal disputes ... on the whole, the sufficient reason for the frankness with which the color line has been drawn in the church is the fact that race discrimination is so respectable an attitude in America that it could be accepted in the church without subterfuge of any sort ... Whether the dogma of white superiority and Negro inferiority has been openly avowed or unconsciously accepted, the white churches have nevertheless taken it for granted and have come to regard it as not incompatible with the remainder of their beliefs.
   >
   > Neibuhr, pp. 236–7

48. Meier, August and Rudwick, Elliott, *The Making of Black America*, vol. I (New York: Atheneum, 1969) p. 186n; Washington and DuBois, *The Negro in the South*, pp. 156–60; 'An Official Report of the Trials of Sundry Negroes charged with an attempt to raise and insurrection in the State of South-Carolina ... prepared and published at the request of the Court', Charleston, 1822, pp. 66–7, published in Aptheker, *Documentary History*, p. 76; see also Aptheker, *Revolts*, pp. 81, 102–3, 209–92.

49. Wilmore, ch. III; Johnson, F. Roy, *The Nat Turner Slave Insurrection*, (Murfreesbro, NC: Johnson Publishing Co., 1966) *passim*; Johnson, F. Roy, *The Nat Turner Story* (Murfreesbro, NC: Johnson Publishing Co., 1970) *passim*; Gray, Thomas R. (ed.), *The Confessions of Nat Turner, the Leader of the Late Insurrection in Southampton*, Baltimore, 1831, partly republished in Aptheker, *Documentary History*, pp. 119–25; Aptheker, *Revolts*, pp. 293–324; Washington and DuBois, *The Negro in the South*, pp. 160–5; Negro Spiritual quoted in Washington, p. 102.

   The following quotation from Raboteau suggests a possible contributing factor to the willingness of slaves to take part in insurrections which were doomed to failure from the start, and as a result of which many would die:

> African slaves in many areas of the New World were convinced that death would free them to return to Africa. This notion was based not simply upon nostalgia for the homeland but upon a firm religious belief in reincarnation. To be properly understood, reincarnation should be placed in the context of the traditional West African conception of the soul as a complex entity – that is, the individual has several spiritual components. One's personality–soul appears before God after death to account for its deeds. When a person sleeps, this soul may wander; dreams are in fact the experiences met by the wandering soul. Linked with the soul is a shadow which is not immortal and dies with the body. Each person also possesses a spirit which serves as a moral guide and which is the Spirit of God within man. It returns to God upon death. There is also a guardian spirit, identified by the Yoruba and the Fon as an ancestor-spirit reincarnated in a descendant. The Yoruba offer sacrifice to the guardian spirit to ensure the propitious development of the person's destiny which the ancestor-spirit has chosen before birth.
>
> Raboteau, p. 32; see also pp. 44–5

Some interesting similarities between African multiple soul concepts and Freud and Jung's models of the mind deserve further investigation. Many of Jung's theories, of course, were developed as a result of his studies in Africa. See also Taylor, pp. 53–6.

50.   DuBois, *The Negro Church*, pp. 25–6; DuBois, *The Negro*, p. 118; Washington and DuBois, *The Negro in the South*, p. 166; see also earlier legislation in Washington and DuBois, pp. 153–5.

51.   Washington, p. 32; Chreitzberg, A. M., *Early Methodism in the Carolinas*, Nashville, Tennessee: np, 1897, pp. 158–9.

52.   Wilmore, pp. 110–14, ch. IV.

53.   Payne, Daniel A., *History of the African Methodist Episcopal Church* (Nashville: Book Concern of the AME Church, 1891) p. 14, in Wilmore, pp. 115–16; Frazier, pp. 32–3; Hamilton, p. 55.

54.   Wilmore, pp. 116–17; Frazier, pp. 33–4.

55.   Wilmore, pp. 116, 118–31.

56.   Raboteau, pp. 178–9, 188–95; Simpson, George Eaton, *Black Religions in the New World* (New York: Columbia University Press, 1978) p. 312.

57.   Raboeau, p. 179; see also pp. 199–207, 209.

58.   DuBois, *The Negro Church*, p. 698; DuBois in Washington and DuBois, *The Negro in the South*, pp. 168–97.

59.   Washington, pp. 33–5; Neibuhr, p. 237. See Lucy McKim Garrison and others quoted in Raboteau, p. 74 and, for example, 'Incidents in the Life of the Rev. J. Asher, Pastor of Shiloh (Coloured) Baptist Church, Philadelphia, United States, and concluding chapter of facts illustrating the unrighteous prejudice existing in the minds of American citizens toward their coloured brethren' (London, 1850) pp. 43–7, republished in Aptheker, *Documentary History*, pp. 189–91.

60.   McKim Garrison, *et al.* in Raboteau, p. 74.

61. Raboteau, pp. 73–4; Wilmore, pp. 150–5.
62. Blyden, Edward W., *Liberia's Offering* (New York: John A. Gray, 1862) pp. 71–2; Carlisle, Rodney, *The Roots of Black Nationalism* (Port Washington, NY: National University Publications, 1975) pp. 77–86; Wilmore, pp. 156–68. For a fuller consideration of the Blyden's life and writings see Lynch, Hollis R., *Edward Wilmott Blyden, Pan-Negro Patriot, 1832–1912* (London: Oxford University Press, 1967) and Lynch, Hollis R., *Black Spokesman: Selected Published Writings of Edward Wilmott Blyden* (London: Frank Cass & Co., 1971).
63. Wilmore, pp. 168–9, 93; see also Hamilton, pp. 110–47.

   Unlike black first generation Pentecostals in Britain, many black American Pentecostals are involved in politics and social action. For example, Mason Temple in Memphis (Church of God in Christ) was the headquarters of the civil rights sanitation workers strike led by Martin Luther King.
64. Frazier, pp. 35–7.
65. Wilmore, pp. 173–86. See also Hollenweger, Walter, J., *Pentecost Between Black and White* (Belfast: Christian Journals Limited, 1974) ch. III.
66. Wilmore, pp. 195–7.
67. Ibid., ch. V, pp. 194, 199; see also Carlisle, pp. 113–16. Marcus Garvey continued in the tradition of Turner and gained many followers for his Universal Negro Improvement Association from among the poor blacks of America who were bitter about their ostracism from the new black middle class, and disillusioned with the traditional black churches. See also Simpson, pp. 124–7.
68. Wilmore, pp. 301–4.
69. Herskovits, pp. xxiv, 232–5.

   In West Africa spiritual power is associated with water, the sea, rivers and streams. The Ashanti, for example, revere Tano the god of that river.
70. Ibid., Raboteau, pp. 56–8. Aptheker, *Revolts*, p. 53. For a consideration of other African retentions see Genovese, Eugene D., *Roll Jordan Roll: the World the Slaves Made* (New York: Pantheon, 1972) pp. 211–24.

   Similar syncretisms have taken place in the Pentecostal type sects in Africa. See for example, Sundkler, Bengt G. M., *Bantu Prophets in South Africa* (Oxford University Press for the International African Institute, 1961) originally Lutterworth Press, 1948) pp. 184–5, 189, 190, 197–8, 200–11, 238–53, 265–75 *passim* and the summary on pp. 262–3. See also Lanternari, pp. 3–62.
71. Davenport, Frederick Morgan, *Primitive Traits in Religious Revivals*, (New York: MacMillan, 1977) pp. 92–3; Herskovits, pp. 227–31; Powdermaker, Hortense, *After Freedom*, (New York: Atheneum, 1969) pp. 259–60, cited in Raboteau, p. 60. See also Beckman, David M., *Black Origins of Possession by the Holy Spirit*, unpublished paper, 1973, pp. 8–13 *passim*. Beckman's writings only became available to me after I had completed research on the black roots of Pentecostalism. He asserts that: 'The only area of the world from which the glossolalia found in Pentecostalism could have possibly been derived is Africa.' Such a claim goes too far. Although the African concept of spirit possession and African spiritual-

ity were crucial, glossolalia was already part of the Christian tradition and is manifest in many other non-European religions. Similarly, Beckman's claim that 'Speaking in tongues is a trance experience. A person in his ordinary state of mind has difficulty even mimicking speaking in tongues', is simply false. Glossolalics may experience altered states of consciousness but few do, and while heightened awareness is common, most Pentecostals and Charasmatics can and do manifest glosslalia during normal consciousness. Beckman, David M. 'Trance from Africa to Pentecostalism' in *Concordia Theological Monthly*, vol. XLV, no. 1, Jan.: 1974, p. 11 *passim*. In spite of these criticisms Beckman's papers contain much useful material on African and black American concepts of spirit possession and, most importantly, recognise the crucial role played by Seymour and other black people in the birth of the Pentecostal movement.

72.   Raboteau, p. 61.
73.   Ibid., p. 72.
74.   See for example the autobiography of AME Bishop, Daniel Alexander Payne, *Recollections of Seventy Years* (New York: Arno Press, 1969; originally 1886) pp. 253–6.
75.   Olmsted, Frederick Law, vol. 1 *The Cotton Kingdom* (New York, 1861) pp. 310–13. See also other examples of black religious motor behaviour in Raboteau, pp. 60–71 and ns 40–64.
76.   See note 75. Mbiti *Philosophy*, p. 82; Herskovits, pp. 211, 216–17; Ellis, A. G., *The Tshi-Speaking Peoples* (London: Chapman & Hall) p. 135; Roscoe, John, *The Baganda* (London: MacMillan, 1911) p. 275; Roscoe, John, *The Bakitara* (Cambridge University Press, 1923) p. 26; Welmers, William E., 'Secret Medicines, Magic, and Rites of the Kpelle Tribe in Liberia' in *The Southwestern Journal of Anthropology*, vol. 5, 1949, p. 232 and Pauwels Marcel, 'Le Culte De Nyabingi (Ruanda)' in *Anthropos*, vol. 46, 1951, p. 355 cited in May, L. Carlyle, 'A Survey of Glossolalia and Other Related Phenomena in Non-Christian Religions' in *American Anthropologist*, vol. 58, 1956, pp. 80, 88, see also p. 84, and accounts of spirit possession in Zimbabwe in Buscher, Herbert *Spirits and Power* (Capetown: Oxford University Press, 1980) pp. 99–100, 153–5 *passim*.
77.   Herskovits, pp. 227–31. White people were also influenced by other practises of African origin. In New Orleans and other locations both black and white were involved with the Voodoo cult throughout most of the nineteenth century. Raboteau, pp. 78, 80.
       James S. Tinney, with some justification, writes concerning Oneness Pentecostalism that: '. . . whites were far more influenced by Black religious culture than were Blacks influenced by whites' and '. . . the persecution white Oneness people have experienced, even at the hands of Trinitarian Pentecostals . . . was largely because of opposition to the Black cultural influences'. Tinney, James S. 'The Significance of Race in the Rise and Development of the Apostolic Pentecostal Movement', in Gill, Jeffery H. (comp.), *Papers Presented to the First Occasional Symposium on Aspects of the Oneness Pentecostal Movement*, (Cambridge, Mass.: Harvard Divinity School, 5–7 July, 1984) p. 63.

78. Herskovits, p. 231. Cf. Synan, Vinson, *The Holiness Pentecostal Movement in the United States* (Grand Rapids, Michigan: William B. Eerdmans Publishing Co., 1961) pp. 21–6; Brown, J. A. C.. *Techniques of Persuasion: from Propaganda to Brainwashing* (Middx: Penguin Books, 1975; originally 1963) ch. 9, pp. 233–43.

    There were also outbursts of glossolalia during many of the eighteenth- and nineteenth-century revivals in the United States. See Eggleston, Edward, *The Circuit Rider: a Tale of the Heroic Age* (New York: Charles Scribner's Sons, 1909) pp. 158–9.

79. Cone, *passim*.

    Some of the earliest hymn writers in the USA were black Pentecostals. See Hollenweger, Walter J. 'A Black Pentenostal Concept: a Forgotten Chapter of Black History: the Black Pentecostals' Contribution to the Church Universal' in *Concept*, no. 50, June 1970, p. 10 esp. n. 11.

80. See also Lucy McKim Garrison *et al.*, quoted in Raboteau, p. 74; Merriam, Alan P., 'Music and the Dance' in Lystad, pp. 452–68.

81. See note 80.

82. Raboteau, pp. 73–4. The nature and degree of African influence on Negro music in the New World has been the focus of considerable debate. DuBois (1903, 1961) Krehbiel (1914), Johnson (1925), Von Hornbostel (1926, 1928), Waterman (1948), Herskovits (1946), and Coutlander (1963), recognised the existence of rhythms, the call and response relationship between leader and chorus and other African elements. Other scholars have stressed the influence of white music – White (1928), Johnson (1930, 1956) and Jackson (1944).

83. Cone, pp. 12–19 *passim*.

    Hollenweger notes that the function of black music and song as a means of communication '. . . was taken up by the Pentecostal revival all over the world where it was really successful be it in Latin America, in the Congo, in Italy, in Indonesia or in Russia' (Hollenweger *Concept*, p. 11). See also Hollenweger, W. J. 'Spirituals' in Davies, J. G. (ed.), *A Dictionary of Liturgy and Worship* (London: SCM Press) pp. 349–50; Mbiti *Introduction*, p. 24 and Miranda, Osmundo Ofonso, *Apocalyptico–Eschatological Hope: a Theology of the Oppressed; an Enquiry into Some Aspects of Popular Black Religion*, unpublished paper, Tuscaloosa, Alabama; Stillman College, 1971.

84. Murphy, Jeanette Robinson, 'The Survival of African Music in America' in *Popular Science Monthly*, New York, 1899, no. 55, pp. 660–72, quoted in Raboteau, p. 145.

85. Cone, pp. 43–4.

86. For a fuller treatment of the way Negro spirituals express both spiritual and political aspirations see Cone, *passim*. Black folk tales had similar functions to those of spirituals. See for example Dorson, *passim*. See also Bascom's consideration of 'verbal art' as a political weapon (Bascom, 'Folklore and Literature' in Lystad, pp. 475–8).

87. Cone, p. 88. A similar view of inaugurated eschatology is to be found in Ladd, George Eldon, *Jesus and the Kingdom* (New York: Harper & Row, 1964; republished as *The Presence of the Future*, London: SPCK, 1980).

88.   Cone, pp. 95–6. The inaugurated eschatology expressed in Negro Spirituals is perhaps related to the African concept of time which is almost two-dimensional, with past and present but virtually no future. Only what has been or can be experienced in history or the present lies within time, while what has not taken place has not been experienced and hence lies outside of time. The future is virtually an extension of the present and is limited to the immediate future of two to six months, and at the most two years. The only future which is recognised 'must be so immediate that people have almost experienced it' (Mbiti, *Philosophy*, pp. 15–28). See also Mbiti, John S., *New Testament Eschatology in an African Background: a Study of the Encounter Between New Testament Theology and African Traditional Concepts* (London: SPCK, 1978; originally Oxford University Press, 1971) *passim*.

89.   For examples of slaves' attitudes towards those who claimed to be Christian yet held them in bondage, see Raboteau, pp. 291–4, 297.

        Many syncretistic African sects also anticipate the arrival of the 'Kingdom' or 'Millenium' when the repressive rule of colonial powers will be overthrown (Lanternari, pp. 3–62, esp. pp. 15, 57).

90.   Cone, pp. 34–5, 44.

91.   Ibid., pp. 45–6; Raboteau, pp. 318, 320.

92.   Cf. Neibuhr, pp. 82–9.

93.   Nelson, Douglas J., *For Such a Time as This: the Story of Bishop William J. Seymour and the Azusa Street Revival*, unpublished Ph.D. dissertation, University of Birmingham, May 1981, pp. 31, 153–8.

94.   Acts 10:34.

CHAPTER 3: THE AMERICAN HOLINESS MOVEMENT

1.   Bruner, Frederick Dale, *A Theology of the Holy Spirit* (London: Hodder & Stoughton, 1970) p. 37.

2.   Anderson, Robert Mapes, *A Social History of the Early Twentieth Century Pentecostal Movement*, Columbia University, Ph.D thesis, 1969 (High Wycombe: University Microfilms, 1972) p. 30. See also McLoughlin's comparison with the tenets of pietistic movements: '... an extremely literalistic reliance upon the Bible, a puritanical morality, pessimistic or escapist outlook on world history, and a perfectionist view of the meaning of salvation' (McLoughlin, William G., *Modern Revivalism: Charles Grandison Finney to Billy Graham* [New York: Ronald, 1959] p. 466).

        Dieter, Melvin E., 'Wesleyan–Holiness Aspects of Pentecostal Origins' in Synan Vinson (ed.), *Aspects of Pentecostal–Charasmatic Origins* (Plainfield, NJ: Logos International, 1975) pp. 62–9.

3.   Wesley, John, *A Plain Account of Christian Perfection* (London: The Epworth Press, 1976) *passim*; Jackson, Thomas (ed.), *The Works of John Wesley* (Grand Rapids, Michigan: Zondervan, 1959) p. 394. Wesley, unlike many of the Holiness advocates who followed in his wake, did not

teach that complete sinless perfection was attainable in this life. Rather, he emphasised that the 'second blessing' would result in the recipient obtaining a 'perfect love' of God and man, and the desire to please God. Nor did Wesley deny, as many of his followers have done, that gradual 'growth in grace' and holiness may also take place.

Hollenweger correctly notes that, 'Classical Pentecostalism ... originated in the encounter of specific Catholic spirituality with the black spirituality of the former slaves in the United States' (Hollenweger, Walter J., 'After Twenty Years' Research on Pentecostalism' in *Theology*, vol. LXXXII, no. 720, Nov. 1984, p. 404).

4. Barbara Zikmund states that the original Oberlin doctrine of sanctification consisted of right willing rather than perfect living, but that: 'Finney distorted Oberlin doctrine with his semi-pelagian confidence in human ability' (Zikmund, Barbara Brown, *Asa Mahn and Oberlin Perfectionism*, Duke University, Ph.D. thesis, 1969 [High Wycombe: University Microfilms, 1970] p. IV).

    Hollenweger, Walter J., *The Pentecostals* (London, SCM Press, 1972) pp. 21, 322. See also Dayton, Donald W., 'Christian Perfection to the Baptism of the Holy Ghost' in Synan, *Aspects*, pp. 41–53; Synan, Vinson, *The Holiness–Pentecostal Movement in the United States* (Grand Rapids, Michigan: William B. Eerdmans Publishing Co., 1961) pp. 26–7.

5. Anderson, p. 31; Synan, *Holiness–Pentecostal*, pp. 28–30. The Holiness institutions were more open to black people and women than those of other traditions.

6. Anderson, p. 32; Synan, *Holiness–Pentecostal*, pp. 33–4.

7. Anderson, p. 33; May, Henry F., *Protestant Churches and Industrial America* (New York: Harper & Bros., 1949) pp. 39–44; Synan, *Holiness–Pentecostal*, p. 31.

8. Anderson, pp. 33–4; Niebuhr, H. Richard, *The Social Sources of Denominationalism* (New York: Living Age Books/Meridan Books, 1957; originally 1929), pp. 34–9, 77–80, 104–5 *passim*.

9. Anderson, pp. 34–5; Synan, *Holiness–Pentecostal*, p. 34. Cf. Niebuhr, pp. 82–9 *passim*.

10. Anderson, pp. 36–7. For a more complete resume of the developments of the post civil war holiness movement see Synan, *Holiness–Pentecostal*, pp. 34–44.

11. Anderson, pp. 34–5; Kuiper, B. K., *The Church in History* (Grand Rapids: William B. Eerdmans Publishing Co., 1951) pp. 470–1. See also Cone, James H., *The Spirituals and the Blues: an Interpretation* (New York: The Seabury Press, 1972) pp. 16f; Synan, *Holiness–Pentecostal*, pp. 56–9; Woodworth-Etter, Harry B., *Signs and Wonders God Wrought in the Ministry for Forty Years* (Chicago: the author, 1916) pp. 145–7, 152–3, quoted in Anderson.

12. Anderson, pp. 41–3; Synan, *Holiness–Pentecostal*, p. 47.

13. Anderson, pp. 42–5. See Synan, *Holiness–Pentecostal*, pp. 44–53 for a more comprehensive account.

14. Synan, *Holiness–Pentecostal*, pp. 61–8, 76. Irwin's 'third blessing' teaching and subsequent appeals for the faithful to seek subsequent baptisms of 'dynamite', 'lydite' and 'oxydite' had some success in North Carolina

and Tennessee where the Church of God (Cleveland) had its beginnings.

15. Anderson, pp. 46–7.
16. Ibid., pp. 47–50; Synan, *Holiness–Pentecostal*, pp. 59–62. For a synopsis of many of the Holiness groups established in the decade after 1894 see Synan, ibid.
17. Dayton, pp. 46–8. The term 'Baptism in the Holy Ghost' had been used occasionally since the early days of Methodism, but the regularity with which the experience of sanctification was so referred to increased until the time of the birth of the Pentecostal Movement. *Baptism of the Holy Ghost* was also the title of Asa Mahan's influential book published in 1870 (Dieter, pp. 65–7).
18. Dayton, pp. 46–51; Dieter, pp. 62–5, 67–73. See also Synan, *Holiness–Pentecostal*, p. 142.
19. Anderson, pp. 50–7, 53n; Torrey, Ruben A., *The Baptism with the Holy Spirit* (New York: Flemming H. Ravell, 1895) pp. 10–15; Menzies, William W., 'Non-Wesleyan Origins of the Pentecostal Movement' in Synan, *Aspects*, pp. 85–8.
20. Anderson, pp. 57–8.
21. Anderson, pp. 57–8.
22. Anderson, pp. 58–62.

CHAPTER 4: CHARLES F. PARHAM AND THE EVIDENCE DOCTRINE

1. Parham, Charles Fox, *A Voice Crying in the Wilderness* (Joplin Printing Co., 1944; originally 1902) pp. 11–19; Parham, Sarah E. (comp.), *The Life of Charles F. Parham: Founder of the Apostolic Faith Movement* (Joplin, Missouri: Tri-State Printing Co.) pp. 1–9, 14, 23–5, 451; Anderson, Robert Mapes, *A Social History of the Early Twentieth Century Pentecostal Movement*, Ph.D. thesis, Columbia University, 1969 (High Wycombe: University Microfilms, 1972) p. 64–9.

   When converted at age thirteen Parham had promised 'the Lord . . . to go to Africa as a missionary' (Parham, *Life*, p. 6; Parham, *Voice*, p. 16).
2. Synan, Vinson, *The Holiness–Pentecostal Movement in the United States* (Grand Rapids, Michigan: William B. Eerdmans Publishing Co., 1971) p. 100.
3. Parham, *Life*, pp. 29, 32–6, 40–6, quotation p. 39. Charles Parham baptised his wife during the early years of his healing ministry. She records that: 'a colored woman on the bank laughed heartily saying: "Look at that there fat woman hugging the preacher." I suppose it would not have been so amusing to her if she had known I was his wife', ibid., p. 36.

   Concerning the medical profession Parham wrote: 'The more proficient in relieving pain a system becomes, the more anti-Christian is its influence . . . the principle drugs used are poisons . . . and medical science stands with fettered hands in the presence of consumption, catarrh, cancers, fevers and many other diseases' (Parham, *Voice*, pp. 40–1). For Parham, salvation included physical healing which was appropriated by faith and was a prerequisite of receiving the baptism of the Holy Spirit (Parham, *Voice*, pp. 46–52).

Seymour also had a negative attitude towards medicine and believed in divine healing but he did not consider it essential for Spirit baptism (*The Apostolic Faith*, vol. I, no. 4, p. 1, col. 1 *passim*).

4. Anderson, p. 71; Parham, *Life*, pp. 37, 39, quotation p. 48. See also Hollenweger, Walter J., *The Pentecostals* (London: SCM Press, 1972) pp. 116–18.

5. Parham, *Life*, pp. 49, 51, 57–8, 70; Parham, *Voice*, pp. 32–3; Anderson, pp. 71–2; *The Apostolic Faith* vol. 1, no. 2, Oct. 1906, p. 1, col. 1.

6. Parham, *Life*, pp. 51–2. Parham believed that those who were baptised with the Holy Spirit would speak in known languages and thus be able to propagate the gospel in foreign lands without the need for language training. In 1902, after the glossolalic experience of the group at 'Stone's Folly', Parham still believed in xenoglossia. He wrote '... how much better it would be for our modern missionaries to obey the injunction of Jesus to tarry for the same power; instead of wasting thousands of dollars, and often their lives in the vain attempt to become conversant in almost impossible tongues which the Holy Ghost could so freely speak. Knowing all languages, He could as easily speak through us one language as another were our tongues and vocal chords surrendered to His domination ...' (Parham, *Voice*, p. 28). For Parham, the Pentecostal experience meant two things: 'The power for witnessing in your own language or any language of the world in this world-wide missionary effort ... and best of all, it seals you unto the day of redemption' (Parham, Charles Fox, *The Everlasting Gospel* [Baxter Springs, Kansas: Robert L. Parham] 1942; originally 1911 p. 29). Parham seems to have taught that only those with the glossolalic baptism or 'sealing' of the Holy Spirit were part of Christ's body – members of the Church. From among that group were others who, because of the 'Israelitish blood in their veins', were members of the 144 000 strong 'Bride' of Christ. From this select group a further elite – 'the Highest Order of Saints' – 'the Man-child' were chosen because their 'perfection is beyond description'. This last group are, according to Parham, to 'rule the nations in the 1000 years reign of Christ' (Parham, *Voice*, pp. 27, 31, 35, 86, 90; Parham, *Everlasting Gospel*, p. 62). In 1911 Parham was still claiming that Spirit baptism enabled the recipient to speak in known languages for the purpose of evangelising foreign lands (Parham, *Everlasting Gospel*, p. 71).

7. Parham, *Life*, p. 52, quotation p. 58; *Apostolic Faith*, ibid.

8. Parham, *Life*, p. 52; Thistlethwaite, Lilian in ibid., p. 59; *The Apostolic Faith*, ibid.

9. Osman, Agnes N., (Mrs N. O. La-Berge) in Parham, *Life*, p. 65.

10. Parham, *Life*, p. 59, quotation pp. 52–3; Parham, *Voice*, p. 34; Anderson, pp. 76–7; *The Apostolic Faith*, ibid.

In her earliest accounts of what happened on that day, Agnes Osman said: 'About three weeks before this while three of us girls were in prayer, I spoke three words in another tongue', quoted in Anderson, pp. 80–1.

11. Thistlethwaite in Parham, *Life*, pp. 60–1. See also *The Apostolic Faith*, ibid.
12. Parham, *Life*, pp. 53–4, 61; Parham, *Voice*, p. 34.
13. Parham, *Life*, pp. 54–5, 62–5; Anderson, pp. 79–81.
14. Anderson, pp. 82–5. Osman, soon after the Los Angeles revival of 1906, had a change of heart and reclaimed her tongues experience. She wrote later that 'I ... was willing to lay down the baptism because of criticism and censure', quoted in Anderson, p. 84n.
15. Parham, *Life*, pp. 88–99; Anderson, pp. 85–9.
16. Parham, *Life*, pp. 99–142. See also Synan, pp. 100–3.

By this time Parham had returned to the practice of believers' baptism. Initially he had rejected baptism, later he practised 'single immersion' but then adopted 'triune immersion'. During his time at 'Stone's Folly' in Kansas, 'the Spirit of God said: "we are buried by baptism into His death ... God the Father, and God the Holy Ghost never died" '. Parham concluded:

> 'we could not be buried by baptism in the name of the Father, and in the name of the Holy Ghost, because it stod for nothing as they never died or were resurrected.' He returned to the practise of baptising 'by single immersion, signifying the death, burial and resurrection; being baptised in the name of Jesus, into the name of the Father, Son and Holy Ghost ...'

Parham's justification for using the name of Jesus in baptism was subsequently adopted and developed by the Oneness branch of the Pentecostal movement (Parham, *Voice*, pp. 21–4).

Parham's *Life* is replete with accounts of xenoglossia but there appears to be no irrefutable evidence that such phenomena were ever demonstrated. In fact, some of the languages claimed don't even exist – 'the Hindoo language', 'the Swedish tongue' etc. (Parham, *Voice*, pp. 54, 116–17, 121–2, 131, *passim*).

Some of the subsequent events in Parham's life are outlined in Chapters 5 and 6.

CHAPTER 5: THE BIRTH OF A MOVEMENT

1. Nelson, Douglas, J., *For Such a Time as This: the Story of Bishop William J. Seymour and the Azusa Street Revival*, unpublished Ph.D. dissertation, University of Birmingham, May 1981, p. 31. Nelson gives a more detailed account of Seymour's early life on pp. 153–8.
2. Ibid., p. 161.
3. Ibid., p. 163; Anderson, Robert Mapes, *A Social History of the Early 20th Century Pentecostal Movement*, Ph.D. thesis, Columbia University, 1969 (High Wycombe: University Microfilms, 1972) pp. 41–3, 152–3.
4. Nelson, pp. 163–4.

5. Ibid., p. 165.
6. Quarles, Benjamin, *The Negro in the Making of America* (New York: Collier, 1964), quoted in Nelson, p. 156.
7. Nelson, pp. 161–3.
8. Nelson, pp. 32–5, 159, 162, 165–7; Parham, Sarah E. (comp.), *The Life of Charles f. Parham: Founder of the Apostolic Faith Movement* (Joplin Missouri: Tri-State Printing Co., 1930) pp. 88–135; Anderson, pp. 64–9.
9. Nelson, p. 35.

    Parham's wife wrote:

    > One colored man, W. J. Seymour, became a regular attendant each day for Bible lessons. In Texas, you know, the colored people are not allowed to mix with the white people, as they do in some other states; but he was so humble and so deeply interested in the study of the Word that Mr. Parham could not refuse him. So he was given a place in the class and eagerly drank in the truths which were so new to him and food to his hungry soul.

    Seymour's 'place in the class' was segregated from whites outside the door, and while he 'drank in the truths' concerning the Holy Spirit baptism, he rejected many of Parham's other teachings including those of racial supremacy (Parham, *Life*, p. 137). Bishop Mack E. Jones, who received the Spirit baptism at Azusa Street in June 1906, recalled that during Parham's subsequent tent meetings in Houston: 'I heard that white and colored was meeting together, but he [Parham] kind of separated the white on one side and colord on another side,' (quoted in Lovett, Leonard, 'Black Origins of the Pentecostal Movement' in Synan, Vinson (ed.), *Aspects of Pentecostal–Charismatic Origins*, [Plainfield, NJ: Logos International, 1975] p. 133).

10. Nelson, p. 168; Anderson, p. 89. See also Synan, Vinson, *The Holiness–Pentecostal Movement in the United States* (Michigan: William B. Eerdmans Publishing Co., 1971) pp. 104–5.
11. Anderson, pp. 93–4; Parham, *Life*, p. 142; Bloch-Hoell, Nils, *The Pentecostal Movement: Its Origin, Development, and Distinctive Character* (Oslo: Universitsforlaget; London: Allen & Unwin, 1964) pp. 30–1. See also Synan, *Holiness–Pentecostal*, pp. 95–8. And the personal account in Bartleman, Frank, *Azusa Street*; originally entitled *How 'Pentecost' Came to Los Angles – How It Was at the Beginning* (Plainfield, NJ: Logos International, 1980; originally 1925) pp. 7–38.
12. Nelson, pp. 187–224.
13. Ibid., p. 188; *The Apostolic Faith*, vol. 1, Sept. 1906, p. 1. col. 1; Anderson, p. 97.
14. Nelson, p. 189; Anderson, pp. 97–8.
15. Nelson, p. 190. The quotation is taken from Acts 2:16.
16. Nelson, p. 191.

    I have observed in Pentecostal congregations that both an individual's initial outburst of glossolalia and many subsequent manifestations are precipitated or 'triggered' by a person – usually of high 'spiritual' status – speaking in glossolalia first. This suggests that some degree of modelling is taking place. See also Florence Crawford's account of her experience at the Azusa Mission, *Light of Life*, pp. 9–10 in Nelson p. 190.

17. Nelson, p. 191. Cf. Niebuhr's description of the character of proletarian religious movements (Niebuhr, H. Richard, *The Social Sources of Denominationalism* [New York: Living Age Books/Meridan Books, 1957; originally 1929] pp. 29–31).

18. Nelson, p. 192.

19. Ibid., pp. 192–4; Anderson, p. 99.

20. Nelson, p. 194.

21. *The Apostolic Faith*, vol I, no. 1, Sept. 1906, p. 1 col. 3. See also Bartleman, pp. 24–5.

22. *Los Angeles Daily Times*, wednesday morning, 19 Apr. 1906, Part II, p. 1. Text reproduced in Nelson, pp. 313–4.

23. *The Apostolic Faith*, vol. 1, no. 1, Sept. 1906, p. 1, col. 1; Bartleman, pp. 47–53; Nelson, p. 196; Anderson, p. 101.

24. *The Apostolic Faith*, op. cit. See also Bartleman, pp. 58–61.

25. Nelson, p. 196.

26. *The Apostolic Faith*, op. cit., p. 3, col. 2.

27. *The Apostolic Faith*, vol. 1, no. 1, Dec. 1906, p. 1.

28. Bishop Mack E. Jones interviewed in 1971 and quoted by Lovett, in Synan, *Aspects*, p. 133.

29. *The Apostolic Faith*, vol. 1, no. 10, Sept. 1907, p. 3, col. 4.

      For a consideration of the place of women as leaders in African societies see Sweetman, David, *Women Leaders in African History* (Heinemann Educational, 1984) *passim*.

30. Hollenweger, Walter J., *The Pentecostals* (London: SCM Press, 1972) p. 24, quoted from a German translation of *Confidence*, Sept. 1912. Also quoted in Nelson, p. 198.

31. Cummings, Mattie, quoted in Nelson, p. 234n.91.

32. Anderson, p. 106.

      In spite of the hostility of many white Holiness ministers towards Seymour, he continued to invite them to preach at the Azusa Mission. See, for example, the account of W. B. Godbey in White, Alma, *Demons and Tongues* (Zarephath, NJ Pillar of Fire, 1949; originally 1936) pp. 119–21.

33. Ibid. pp. 107–9. Nickel, Thomas, R., *The Amazing Shakarian Story* (Los Angeles: Full Gospel Business Men's Fellowship International, 1964).

34. For a partial list of other early Pentecostal periodicals – some seventy-four of which were published in the United States – see Anderson, pp. 116–17.

35. Anderson, p. 110.

36. Ibid., pp. 115–16; *The Apostolic Faith*, vol. 2, no. 13, May 1908, *passim*.

37. Nelson, pp. 213–14; Bartleman, pp. 53–4. For a fuller account of American missionaries leaving from the Azusa mission see Anderson, pp. 108–12.

      Many Negroes were among the missionaries who went to foreign fields – particularly Africa – or spread the movement throughout the United States. Reporting the Pentecostal Movement's spread to New York, the

New York American of 3 Dec. 1906, declared that it was: 'Led by a negro, calling himself Elder Sturdevant, who comes here from Los Angeles en route to the interior of Africa. . . . The leaders of this strange movement are for the most part negroes and of the poor and uneducated class, but some at least of the converts made here are people of refinement and culture' (quoted in Bloch-Hoell, Nils, *The Pentecostal Movement* [Oslo, Universitetsforlaget; London: Allen & Unwin, 1964], p. 49).

38.   Synan, *Holiness–Pentecostal*, pp. 122–33; *The Apostolic Faith*, vol. I, no. 4, Dec. 1906, p. 3, cols 1–2.

39.   Synan, *Holiness–Pentecostal*, pp. 123–33.

40.   Tomlinson, A. J., *The Last Great Conflict*, (Cleveland: Press of Walter E. Rodgers, 1913) pp. 211, 214, quoted in Stone, James, *The Church of God of Prophecy, History and Polity* (Cleveland: White Wing Publishing House and Press, 1977) p. 27; Synan, *Holiness–Pentecostal*, pp. 133–4; Tomlinson, Homer A., (ed.), *Diary of A. J. Tomlinson* (New York: Church of God World Headquarters, 1949–1955, vol. I; pp. 17–18, vol. III: p. 49. Dugger, Lillie, *A. J. Tomlinson* (Cleveland, Tennessee: White Wing Publishing House, 1964) pp. 52–3; Conn, Charles W., *Like a Mighty Army: a History of the Church of God* (Cleveland: Pathway Press, 1977) pp. 84–5.

Cashwell, unable to dominate the Pentecostal movement he had helped to create in the South, defected in 1909 and returned to the Methodist Church. Synan, *Holiness–Pentecostal*, p–138–9.

41.   Synan, *Holiness–Pentecostal*, pp. 135–7.

Many of the ministers who founded the white Assemblies of God in 1914 had been ordained by Bishop Mason and issued with Church of God in Christ credentials. Ibid. pp. 169–70.

42.   Nelson, p. 216.

43.   Ibid..

44.   Ibid. pp. 64, 217–18.

45.   Ibid. p. 218.

CHAPTER 6: THE RE-DRAWING OF THE COLOUR LINE

1.   *The Apostolic Faith* (Baxter Springs, Kansas, Apr. 1925) pp. 9, 10; Parham, Sarah E. (comp.) *The Life of Charles F. Parham Founder of the Apostolic Faith Movement* (Joplin, Missouri: Tri-State Printing Co., 1930) pp. 148, 154–5, 160, 168.

2.   Parham, Charles F., *A Voice Crying in the Wilderness* (Baxter Springs, Kansas: Joplin Printing Co., 1944) pp. 83, 91–100; Parham, *Life*, p. 163; Parham, Charles, Fox, *The Everlasting Gospel* (Baxter Springs, Kansas: np, 1942; originally 1911) p. 72; Parham, *Life*, pp. 163–4; Nelson, Douglas J. *For Such a Time as This: the Story of Bishop William J. Seymour and the Azusa Street Revival*, unpublished Ph.D. dissertation, University of Birmingham, May 1981, p. 209. Parham also claimed that at the Azusa Mission people 'were taught to yield to any force . . . hypnotic influence

... spooks' false spirits and demons Parham, *Everlasting Gospel*, ibid).
Parham also wrote that at Azusa:

> many forms of fanaticism have crept in ... I found hypnotic
> influences, familiar–spirit influences, spiritualistic influences, mes-
> meric influences, and all kinds of spells, spasms, falling in trances, etc.
> All of these things are foreign to and unknown in this movement
> outside of Los Angeles, except in the places visited by the workers sent
> out from this city ... the Holy Ghost does nothing that is unnatural or
> unseemingly [sic], and any strained exertion of body, mind, or voice is
> not the work of the Holy Spirit .... The Holy Ghost never leads us
> beyond the point of self-control ...
>
> (Ibid., pp. 168–70)

4.   Parham, *Voice*, pp. 81–3; Parham, *Everlasting Gospel*, pp. 1–3 ; Nelson,
      p. 242. Examples of Parham's continuing hostility to Seymour and
      Azusa appear in Parham, *Everlasting Gospel*, pp. 71–2.
5.   Parham, *Voice*, p. 84; Parham, *Everlasting Gospel*, p. 4.
6.   Parham, *Voice*, pp. 106–7. Parham's views were far from original. In the
      main he was repeating the teachings of the 'British Israel' movement
      which developed the theory that the British and 'kindred peoples'
      were the descendants of the ten tribes of the house of Israel which had
      been taken into captivity in Assyria. There was ambivalence in the
      movement regarding the significance of the identification of the Anglo-
      Saxons with Israel. Some, like Parham, clearly believed themselves to
      be members of a a superior race – the master race – while others saw
      themselves as 'the servant people' who would lead other nations into the
      blessings of the Gospel. Particularly influential were the writings of
      Dennis Hanan and H. Aldersmith. Their book *British Israel Truth*
      became known as the 'Handbook' of the movement and ran into
      thirteen editions (37 000) between 1891 and 1926. British Israel beliefs
      were widespread in the British Pentecostal Movement but only found
      official favour in the Bible Pattern Church (two-stage) and, more
      recently, in the Church of God in Ireland (Oneness). Since the Second
      World War the movement has been in decline and only receives support
      from a few elderly middle class patriots. One independent Pentecostal
      preacher in Britain, Brian Williams, still attempts to promote these
      teachings in Britain and South Africa as does the Church of God/
      Ambassador College of Herbert W. Armstrong in the United States
      (Williams, Brian, *Britain's Royal Throne* (Birmingham: Brian Williams
      Evangelistic Association, 1968); Armstrong, Herbert, W., *The United
      States and British Commonwealth in Prophecy* (Pasadena, California:
      Ambassador College Press, 1972).
      Parham's British Israelite beliefs are summarised in Parham, *Voice*,
      pp. 92–100, 105–18.
7.   *The Apostolic Faith*, vol, 1, no. 4, Dec. 1906, p. 1, col. 2.
      Parham held to the Conditionalist view of personal eschatology which
      was rejected by most Pentecostals.
8.   Nelson, pp. 211, 242n.151. According to Alma White, 'Parham's
      company said Seymour's people had the devil in them' White, Alma,

Demons and Tongues [Zarephath, New Jersey: Pillar of Fire, 1949; originally 1936] p. 81.

9. Parham, *Life*, p. 276; Synan, Vinson, *The Holiness–Pentecostal Movement in the United States* (Grand Rapids, Michigan: William B. Eerdmans Publishing Co., 1971) p. 180; *Apostolic Faith* (Baxter Springs, Kansas, Missouri, Mar. 1927) p. 5 quoted in Anderson; Robert Mapes, *A Social History of the Early Twentieth Century Pentecostal Movement* (Columbia University, Ph.D.) dissertation, 1969 (High Wycombe: University Microfilms) pp. 320–1.

10. Anderson, p. 321. See also Synan, pp. 180–1.

11. White, *Demons and Tongues*, pp. 72–3; Bartleman, Frank, *Azusa Street* (Plainfield NJ: Logos International, 1980; originally 1925) p. 84; Synan, *Holiness–Pentecostal*, p. 111.

Alma White was particularly hostile towards Seymour. He had visited her in the spring of 1906, while on his way to Los Angeles. She later wrote that:

> His appearance aroused my curiosity and at the close of the meal I called on him to pray. He responded with a good deal of fervor, but before he had finished I felt that serpents and other climy creatures were creeping all around me. After he had left the room, a number of the students said they felt he was devil possessed .... In my evangelistic and missionary tours I had met all kinds of religious fakirs and tramps, but I felt that he excelled them all ... It was said that God raised up a colored man to bring Pentecost back to earth again ... but they [Seymour's followers and other Pentecostals] were carried away in the most hellish outburst of demoniacal power that has ever been known under the name of religion.
>
> White, *Demons*, pp. 67–8, 70

White's hostility towards Seymour was at least partly motivated by her racist upbringing in Kentucky. While a teacher in Utah, she had two black children in her class and would have refused to teach them had she not feared the loss of her job as a result. She believed that members of the school staff had arranged to 'impose the colored children upon' her in order to cause her offence (White, Alma, *Looking Back from Beulah* [Zarepath, New Jersey: Pillar of Fire, 1951; originally 1902] pp. 87–8.

In 1924 the Norwegian, Emanuel Linderholm, reflected White's negative view of Seymour when he wrote: 'It is also possible that there has been something demonic about this negro, which in itself, anymore than with Rasputin, should not have hindered, but rather promoted his suggestive influence, especially within the female world' (Linderholm, Emanuel, *Pirgstroreisen.1 Dess forutststtningar och upppkomst. Ekstas, under och apokalyptik i bibel och nytida folkreligiositet* [Stockholm, 1924] p. 244, quoted in Bloch-Hoell, Nils, *The Pentecostal Movement* (Oslo: Universitetsforlaget; London: Allen & Unwin, 1964) pp. 36–7.

12. *Confidence*, June 1911, p. 139.

13. Durham, taught that the words of Christ on the cross: 'It is finished', meant that not only was the work for man's salvation completed but

also the work for man's sanctification. However the movement which followed Durham's teaching generally emphasised the progressive nature of sanctification rather than the instant eradication of sin at conversion. Anderson, pp. 280–1.

14. Nelson, p. 247; Synan, *Holiness–Pentecostal*, p. 148. Some understood Durham as teaching progressive sanctification as opposed to a second experience or work of grace, but Durham maintained, like Count Zinzendorf of the Moravians and Charles G. Finney, that sanctification was completed at conversion. See Nelson, pp. 276–8ns6, 7.

15. Nelson, p. 247; Anderson, p. 282; Synan, *Holiness–Pentecostal*, pp. 148–9.

16. Nelson, p. 248; Menzies, William W., 'Non Wesleyan Origins of the Pentecostal Movement' in Synan, Vinson, *Aspects of Pentecostal–Charasmatic Origins* (Plainfield, NJ: Logos International, 1975) pp. 90–2.

17. Nelson, pp. 248–52. *The Apostolic Faith, passim.*

18. Anderson, pp. 317–18; Bloch-Hoell, Nils, *The Pentecostal Movement* (Oslo: Universitetsforlaget; London: Allen & Unwin, 1964) pp. 53–4.

19. Nelson, pp. 208–11.

20. Ibid., p. 255.

21. Synan, *Holiness–Pentecostal*, p. 170. See also ibid., p. 152–3.

22. Ibid., p. 153.

23. Anderson, pp. 283–4, 318; Menzies, pp. 92–4.

The majority of Second Work (or three-stage) Pentecostals were concentrated in the rural agrarian Southern States, while most of the Finished Work (or two-stage) Pentecostals were to be found in urban areas. During the early years of the Pentecostal Movement most white Pentecostal congregations outside the South had no recognised religious body to ordain their ministers and, in consequence, they could not perform marriages or obtain concessionary railway fares. The black church of God in Christ had been legally incorporated in 1897 and became Pentecostal after one of its leaders, C. H. Mason, visited the Azusa Mission in 1907. Between 1907 and 1914 the Church of God in Christ issued credentials to hundreds of white ministers. Their attachment to Mason's organisation was purely nominal and did not lead to an interracial fellowship. In 1912, Mason allowed a group of white ministers in Texas and Alabama to issue credentials in the name of the Church of God in Christ but signed by their own leaders. These leaders were H. A. Goss, D. C. Opperman, H. G. Rodgers and A. C. Collins. In 1914 these men were responsible for the calling of the convention at Hot Springs, Arkansas at which was founded the Assemblies of God. How could these white Pentecostals reject their black co-religionists when they had so consistently shown love and concern for their well-being? How could they resolve their feelings of guilt at creating a rival all white organisation? Some powerful rationalising must have taken place in attempts to justify their actions.

24. Pentecostals who adhered to the Finished Work view stressed two experiences or stages: conversion and the baptism of the Holy Spirit. Consequently they are designated as 'two-stage Pentecostals'. Those who emphasised the original Wesleyan–Holiness doctrine of a second work of grace are designated as 'three-stage Pentecostals'.

These terms were coined by Walter Hollenweger in his ten-volume *Handbuch der Pfingstbewegung* (Geneva) 1965–67, and are also used in Hollenweger, *The Pentecostals* (London: SCM Press, 1972) pp. 324–5; Synan, *Holiness–Pentecostal*, pp. 79–80, 167–70 and Anderson, pp. 284–7.

25. Ibid., pp. 284–6. See also Synan, *Holiness–Pentecostal*, pp. 149–50.

26. This would include Baptists, Presbyterians and those advocating the Keswick view of holiness.

27. Anderson, pp. 287, 293; Lovett, Leonard, 'Black Origins of the Pentecostal Movement' in Synan, *Aspects*, op. cit., p. 127.

Although many of the early black Pentecostal leaders had come from a Baptist background, they generally subscribed to the Wesleyan–Holiness view of sanctification as being a second work of grace. On the other hand most white Baptists subscribed to the Reformed view of sanctification as a continuous and ongoing process.

28. Anderson, p. 294.

29. Ibid., p. 317. See also Synan, *Holiness–Pentecostal*, pp. 167–174; Hollenweger, Walter J. 'A Black Pentecostal Concept' in *Concept*, no. 50, June 1970, p. 41.

30. Conn, Charles, W., *Like a Mighty Army: a History of the Church of God* (Cleveland: Pathway Press, 1977) pp. 132–3.

31. Tomlinson, A. J., *Journal of Happenings*, manuscript diary of A.J. Tomlinson in the Archives of the Church of God, Cleveland, Tennessee, 1901–23, quoted in Synan, *Holiness–Pentecostal*, p. 173.

This entry is omitted from the published *Diary of A. J. Tomlinson*, vol. 1, 1901–23 (New York: The Church of God, World Headquarters) 1949.

32. Conn, p. 133.

33. Tomlinson, A. J., *Minutes of the Sixteenth Assembly* (Cleveland, Tennessee, 1926) pp. 25–6.

34. Anderson, pp. 321–2. Synan, *Holiness–Pentecostal*, pp. 173–4. In 1966, the Church of God abolished its separate 'coloured assembly', deleted all references to colour from its minutes and integrated the black congregations (*Minutes of the 51st General Assembly* (Cleveland, Tennessee, 1966) p. 62.

35. Nelson, pp. 261–3.

36. Seymour, W. J., *Amended Articles of Incorporation*, 19 May, 1914, p. 1, quoted in Nelson, p. 264.

37. Ibid., p. 4.

38. Seymour, W. J., *Doctrine and Discipline of the Azusa Street Apostolic Faith Mission*, p. 10, quoted in Nelson, p. 265.

39. Nelson, p. 271.

40. For a more extensive treatment of the Oneness doctrines see Reed, David Arthur, *Origins and Development of the Theology of Oneness Pentecostalism in the US*, unpublished Ph.D. dissertation, Boston University, 1978.

Oneness Pentecostals assert that:

Matthew 28:19 was a command by Jesus to baptize in the NAME. The Apostles did not repeat the words of the command, but they did obey it (Acts 2:38; 8:16; 10:48; 4:12; Col. 3:17).... Since Father, Son, and Holy Ghost are titles or manifestations of the Almighty Spirit and His body, the Apostles understood His SAVING NAME to be JESUS

.... THE NAME OF THE FATHER, SON, AND HOLY GHOST
IS LORD JESUS CHRIST.
Manuwal, Lewis, *Water Baptism According to the Bible and Historical
References* (Hazelwood, Missouri: End-time Ministries, nd.) p. 5

41.   A 'proof text' often used to support this position is John 3:5.
The debate between the Oneness and Trinitarian Pentecostals was
predicated on a simplistic and hence erroneous understanding of the
early trinitarian creeds and formulae. The term 'persona', translated as
'person' was understood by Pentecostals in its modern sense. Thus the
statement that God 'eternally exists in three persons, God the Father,
God the Son and God the Holy Ghost', suggested to them that God was
three self-conscious beings. The Oneness Pentecostals – with some
justification – accused the Trinitarians of tri-theism and maintained that
'there is only one Person in the Godhead' and that in Jesus 'dwelleth all
the fullness of the Godhead bodily'. We believe that 'Jesus was Mary's
son and Mary's God, Creator and creature, God manifest in the flesh ...
that Jesus was the Eternal Father made visible apart from whom there is
no God' (Clanton, Arthur L. *United We Stand* [Hazelwood, Missouri: The
Pentecostal Publishing House, 1970] pp. 142–3; *Minutes Book of the
Pentecostal Assemblies of the World, Inc.* np, 1981).
Friedrich Schleiermacher, a rather more sophisticated theologian,
shared some of the anti-trinitarian, modalistic views of Oneness
Pentecostals, and Karl Barth, who is not a modalist, has recognised the
obsolescence of the world 'person' and the problems raised by the
modern sense of the term. Consequently, he speaks of three 'modes of
being. ... The Father is disclosed in the Son and communicated in the
Spirit. ... The God who reveals Himself according to Scripture is One
in three of His own modes of existence, which consist in their mutual
relationsips, Father, Son, and Holy Spirit' (Schleiermacher, Friedrich,
D. E., *The Christian Faith* (English trans. of the Second German edn), T.
and T. Clarke, 1968, pp. 738–51; Barth, Karl *Church Dogmatics*, (English
trans.), vol. 1, i, pp. 300–400).
Cone, writing of Negro Spirituals, notes that,

... statements about God are not theologically distinct from
statements about Jesus Christ. ... There are no theories about the
'ousia' or Being of the Son in relation to the Father. (It is safe to
assume that black slaves did not know about the proceedings of Nicea
and Chalcedon.). ... For black slaves, Jesus is God himself breaking
into man's historical present and transforming it according to divine
expectations.

The songs of the slave community approximated more closely to a
Oneness/Jesucentric position than a trinitarian one (Cone, James, H.
The Spirituals and the Blues: an Interpretation (New York: The Seabury
Press, 1972).
The theology of Oneness rejects the platonic presuppositions of
trinitarianism in favour of a distinctly Hebraic perspective which has
much in common with the world view of West Africa (Reed, David

'Aspects of the Origins of Oneness Pentecostalism' in Synan, *Aspects*, pp. 145–7).

42. See also Gill, Jeffrey (ed.), *Papers Presented to the First Occasional Symposium on Aspects of the Oneness Pentecostal Movement*, held at Harvard Divinity School, Cambridge, Massachusetts, 5–7 July 1984.

The Oneness Pentecostals teach a form of baptismal regeneration. The 'one baptism' is in 'two elements ... we are baptised into Jesus Christ in WATER and the HOLY SPIRIT' and 'the Bible standard of full salvation', according to the white United Pentecostal Church, 'is repentance, baptism in water by immersion in the name of the Lord Jesus Christ, and the baptism of the Holy Ghost with the initial sign of speaking with other tongues as the Spirit gives utterance'. In the preface to a King James version of the Bible published by the UPC in 1973, it states: '... the baptism of the Holy Ghost, with the evidence of speaking in other tongues, identifies us with Christ in His resurrection (Romans 6:5 and Romans 8:11). Just as Jesus Christ experienced death, burial, and resurrection in providing our salvation, we experience a type of death, burial, and resurrection in receiving salvation through the steps of repentance, baptism in Jesus' name, and the infilling of the Holy Ghost' (Campbell, David 'Baptism in Two Elements' in *Pentecostal Truth*, vol. 1, no. 8, June, 1973, p. 7; *What We Believe and Teach: Articles of Faith of the United Pentecostal Church* [St. Louis, Missouri, nd, p. 7]; *The Holy Bible* [Hazelwood, Missouri: World Aflame Press, 1973] p. 9

Similarly, the 'Doctrine' of the predominantly black Pentecostal Assemblies of the World states that: 'We believe that everyone must be born again to enter into the Kingdom of God. (St. John 3: 3, 5) We further believe that to experience the new birth one must be baptised with the Holy Spirit (Ghost) with the initial evidence of speaking in tongues as the Spirit of the Lord giveth utterance' (*Minute Book of the Pentecostal Assemblies of the World, Inc.* [1981] p. 21).

For most – though by no means all – Oneness Pentecostals, particularly many white Americans of the UPC, it is simply a case of 'tongues or hell' – those who have not experienced Spirit baptism evidenced by glossolalia, are not saved. Many of the UPC members in Britain are less than convinced concerning this doctrine.

For a more extensive treatment of the soteriological significance of Spirit baptism in the United Pentecostal Church see Lewis, Dan, 'The Theology of the Baptism in the Holy Spirit in the United Pentecostal Church' in Gill, pp. 196–231.

James S. Tinney correctly notes that in Oneness Pentecostalism: 'Additional Black or African influences can be witnessed in the emphasis on monotheism, in the belief that the Spirit is an influence or force rather than a person, in the insistence on the magical use of the name, in the restoration of the primacy of the ritual use of water, in the rejection of the major Western Christian concept of justification by faith alone, and in the value placed on subjective revelation' (Tinney, James S. 'The Significance of Race in the Rise and Development of the Apostolic Pentecostal Movement' in Gill, p. 58).

43. Ewart, Frank, J. *The Phenomenon of Pentecost* (St Louis: Pentecostal

Publishing House, 1947), pp. 75–6; Reed, David, 'Aspects of the Origins of Oneness Pentecostalism' in Synan, *Aspects*, pp. 145–9.

The development of 'Jesus name' theology was to a great extent the logical conclusion of the Jesucentric perspective or revivalistic fundamentalism in the United States.

44. Anderson, pp. 297, 299; Reed, Ibid.; Golder, Morris E., *History of the Pentecostal Assemblies of the World* (Indianopolis, Indiana: PA of W, 1973) pp. 43–5. See also Synan, *Holiness–Pentecostal*, pp. 153–6.

45. Clanton, pp. 21–2; Anderson, pp. 300–7; Menzies, pp. 94–5. See also Synan, *Holiness–Pentecostal*, pp. 156–8.

46. Anderson, pp. 309–3.

47. Ibid., p. 319; Synan, *Holiness–Pentecostal*, pp. 170–1.

Roswith Gerloff records an undocumented story related by Monroe R. Saunders. During the 1916 General Council Meeting between the advocates of Oneness and Trinitarianism, '... a man from Georgia, where killing and lynching of Blacks were daily experience ... began to shout at the Blacks: "I'm from Georgia!" Peter J. F. Bridges from the Eastern States, a Pentecostal Black pioneer, a prolific and convincing speaker, and very ugly, rose to his feet on the other side: "And I'm Peter Jan Bridges from New York, and I want you to know that I couldn't care less if you came from hell!' " (Gerloff, Roswith, I. H., 'Blackness and Oneness (Apostolic) Theology: Cross Cultural Aspects of a Movement' in Gill, p. 88).

48. Anderson, pp. 319–20. See also Howell's somewhat biased account of the events leading up to the AOG, Oneness split.

Howell, Joseph, ' "Jesus Rediscovered" The New Issue in the Assemblies of God' in Gill.

After the death of Seymour, the white AOG were asked if they wanted to purchase Seymour's Azusa Street Mission. They declined, saying that they were not interested in relics (Bloch-Hoell, Nils, *The Pentecostal Movement* [Oslo: Universitetsforlaget; London: Allen & Unwin, 1964] p. 139.

49. Haywood, G. T., *A Voice Crying in the Wilderness*, vol. 2, no. 9, 1921, cited in Golder, p31.

50. Golder, pp. 31–2.

51. Haywood, *Voice*, 1921, quoted in Golder, p. 36.

52. Clanton, pp. 23, 25; Golder, pp. 46–7; Foster, Fred J. *Think It Not Strange: a History of the Oneness Movement* (St Louis, Missouri: Pentecostal Publishing House, 19) p. 73.

53. Clanton, pp. 25–6; Foster, p. 74.

54. Golder, pp. 45–50; Clanton, pp. 27–8.

55. Clanton, p. 28.

56. Foster, p. 74.

57. Golder, pp. 48–50; Clanton, pp. 27–8; Foster, p. 74.

58. McClain, S. C., unpublished notes quoted in Clanton, p. 28.

59. McClain, S. C., unpublished notes quoted in Foster, p. 74.

60. Golder, p. 65.

61. Golder, p. 67.

62. Golder, p. 67, quotation p. 70, see also p. 79.

63. Foster, pp. 75–6; Clanton, pp. 29–30.
64. Golder, pp. 77–9.
65. Golder, p. 78.
66. Quoted in Golder, pp. 78–9.
67. Ibid., pp. 78–9.
68. Clanton, pp. 31–2.
69. Kidson, W. E., *The Apostolic Herald*, July, 1930, p. 5. Quoted in Clanton.
70. McClain, pp. 24–5, quoted in Foster, p. 76; Clanton, pp. 33, 35–127; Golder, pp. 82–3; Foster, pp. 77–89.
71. Clanton, p. 28.
72. McClain, quoted in Foster, p. 74; Clanton, p. 32; Foster, pp. 74–5.
73. Clanton, p. 32.
74. Golder, pp. 83–93.
75. Ibid. pp. 96–120; Clanton, pp. 84–86.
    Changing from an 'episcopal' to a 'presbyterian' form of church government meant that the black bishops had their power limited and leadership became white and bureaucratic rather than black and charasmatic.
76. Hollenweger, Walter J. *Pentecost Between Black and White: Five Case Studies on Pentecost and Politics*, Belfast: Christian Journals Ltd., 1974, pp. 20–1.

CHAPTER 7: BLACK BIRTH, INTERRACIAL INFANCY

1. Synan, Vinson, *The Holiness–Pentecostal Movement in the United States* (Grand Rapids, Michigan: William B. Eerdmans Publishing Co., 1961) p. 168.
2. Quotation from Tinney, James S., *Competing Theories of Historical Origins for Black Pentecostalism*, paper presented at the Annual Meeting of the American Academy of Religion, 16 Nov. 1979, New York City, p. 6; Tinney, James S., 'William J. Seymour: Father of Modern Day Pentecostalism' in the *Journal of the Interdenominational Theological Center*, Atlanta, Georgia, vol. 4, 1976, p. 34; Tinney, James S., 'Black Origins of the Pentecostal Movement' in *Christianity Today*, 8 Oct. 1971.
3. Quotation from Lovett, Leonard, 'Black Origins of the Pentecostal Movement' in Synan, Vinson (ed.), *Aspects of Pentecostal–Charasmatic Origins* (Plainfield, NJ: Logos International, 1975) p. 138; Lovett, Leonard, 'Perspectives on the Black Origins of the Contemporary Pentecostal Movement' in the *Journal of the Interdenominational Theological Center*, op. cit., vol. 1, 1973, pp. 42–6. David Beckman has also written on the black origins of Pentecostalism. See Beckman, David M., *Black Origins of Possession by the Holy Spirit*, unpublished paper, 1973, and Beckman, David M. 'Trance from Africa to Pentecostalism' in *Concordia Theological Monthly*, vol. 45, no. 1, Jan. 1874, pp. 11–26. The *New York American*, 3 Dec. 1906, repoerted that 'The leaders of this strange movement are for the most part Negroes', quoted in Hollenweger, Walter J., 'A Black Pentecostal Concept, A Foreign Chapter of Black History: the Black Pentecostals' Contribution to the Church Universal', in *Concept*, no. 50, June 1970, p. 13.

4. Synan, *Holiness–Pentecostal, passim*. See also Kelsey, Morton, T. *Tongues Speaking* (New York: Doubleday, 1961) pp. 64–5; Nelson, Douglas J., *For Such a Time as this: the Story of Bishop William J. Seymour and the Azusa Street Revival*, unpublished Ph.D. dissertation, University of Birmingham, May 1981, *passim*.

5. Hollenweger, Walter J., *The Pentecostals* (London: SCM Press, 1972) pp. 23–4; originally in his ten-volume *Handbuch der Pfingstbewegung* (Geneva) 1965–67. See also Hollenweger, *Concept*, pp. 11–17. Hollenweger's recognition of the black origins of the Pentecostal movement is particularly perceptive since it was made in 1965 and based exclusively on white sources. This assessment of origins which was mainly intuitive has been upheld by subsequent research. Conversation with W. J. Hollenweger, 21 Dec. 1984.

6. *The Apostolic Faith*, vol. 1, no. 1, Sept. 1906, p. 3, col. 2; ibid., vol. 1, no. 4, Dec. 1906, p. 1, cols 2, 5; The *Kansas City Journal*, 22 Jan. 1901 describing Parham's ministry referred to the 'Gift of Tongues' but reported that: 'In many respects it recalled an old-fashioned Methodist prayer meeting.' Quoted in Parham, Sarah E. (comp.), *The Life of Charles F. Parham: Founder of the Apostolic Faith Movement* (Joplin, Missouri: Tri-State Printing Co., 1930) pp. 71–2..

7. *Los Angeles Daily Times*, Wednesday morning, 18 Apr. 1906, Part II, p. 1, text reproduced in Nelson pp. 313–14, and Bartleman, Frank *Azusa Street* (Plainfield, NJ: Logos International, 1980) pp. 175–6.

8. *Apostolic Faith* (Baxter Springs, Kansas, Apr. 1925) pp. 9–10, quoted in Anderson, Robert Mapes, *A Social History of the Early Twentieth Century Pentecostal Movement*, Ph.D. thesis, Columbia University, 1969 (High Wycombe: University Microfilms, 1972) p. 320. Parham made it clear that when the glossolalic manifestations occurred in 1901 at his College of Bethel, 'There was no violent physical manifestation, though some trembled under the power of the glory that filled them.' Everything, he stressed was done with 'propriety and decency' (Parham, *Life*, pp. 53, 55, 144, 155–6). Later, in 1911, he wrote: 'Two-thirds of this tongue stuff over the country is not Pentecost. The counterfeits have no real languages, and fleshly controls of spiritualistic origin have destroyed their soul saving power.' He also implicitly recognised the African influences at the Azusa Mission when he scathingly wrote: 'The Pentecostal Assemblies originated in a negro mission in Los Angeles, California, and is a cross between the old-fashioned negro worship of the South, and Holy-Rollerism' (Parham, Charles Fox, *The Everlasting Gospel* [Baxter Springs, Kansas: Robert L. Parham, 1942; originally 1911] pp. 31, 118.

    Similarly, his wife writing of the events in 1901 stated that: 'The experience they received was very different to what many today consider Pentecostal power. There was no yelling and screaming with violent physical exertion and consequent exhaustion. There was no nervous strain in connection with any of the demonstrations.' She also claimed that Seymour wrote to her husband 'appealing for help, as spiritualistic manifestations, hypnotic forces and fleshly contortions as known in the colored Camp Meetings in the south, had broken loose in the meeting,'

(Parham, *Life*, pp. 53, 55, 155–6).

Another severe critic of Azusa Street, Nettie Harwood, described what was probably African motor behaviour when she reported witnessing: 'A young colored woman, doing her best to get the gibberish, went through all kinds of muscular contortions in her efforts to get her tongue to work' (White, Alma, *Demons and Tongues* [Zarepath, New Jersey: Pillar of Fire, 1949; originally 1936] p. 72).

Although Parham's meetings were extremely restrained, this was not the norm among early Pentecostals. Ambrose Jessup Tomlinson, for example, reported: 'Men, Women, children screaming, shouting, praying, leaping, dancing and falling prostrate on the straw. Wonderful' (Tomlinson, Ambrose Jessup, *Diary of A. J. Tomlinson.* vol. 1, 1901 to 1923 [New York: The Church of God, World Headquarters, 1949] p. 98 *passim*).

Motor behaviour which was essentially West African in origin, continued to be manifest by both black and white Pentecostals throughout the early years of the movement. In 1909, Frederic G. Henke wrote a description of a Pentecostal meeting in Chicago based on his visits to five places of worship:

> ... the leader ... has been praying for the meeting; for he must be positive that the Spirit has taken entire possession of him before he takes part. His evidence of the presence of the Spirit appears to be the violent jerking of his head. ... by this time, automatic movements of the head actually appear in various parts of the house, the tendency being for others to immitate the leader or those who are most pronounced in their demonstrations. ... A coloured man rises and gives a rousing testimony. ... At once there is a response from all over the house (about three hundred are present), some shouting, some manifesting violent jerks, some screaming, and some laughing aloud. ... Arms move frantically, heads jerk so violently that some of the women are unable to keep their hats on ... a girl in the meeting so looses her inhibitions that she jerks all over. ... A woman at the altar throws herself upon the floor and writhes as though in the most excruciating pain.
> Henke, Frederic G; 'The Gift of Tongues and Related Phenomena at the Present Day' in *American Journal of Theology*, vol. XIII, 1909, pp. 196–7

9.   *The Apostolic Faith*, vol. 1, no. 4, Dec. 1906, p. 1, col. 4. The idea of being possessed by the Holy Spirit was not limited to black Pentecostalism. Frank Bartleman, an early white Pentecostal, expressed the same belief: 'My mind, the last fortress of man to yield was taken possession of by the Spirit ... was possessed of Him fully. ... We want the Holy Ghost, but the fact is He is wanting possession of us. ... The Pentecostal baptism spells complete abandonment, possession by the Holy Ghost, of the whole man, with a spirit of obedience' (Bartleman, pp. 72–3).

10. Matthew 24:15.

11. Parham, *Life*, pp. 51–4. Parham apparently taught that a person could not receive the baptism of the Holy Spirit as long as they were physically

ill. 'Let your bodies be clean. You cannot receive the gift of the Holy Spirit unless you are clean. Catarrh, consumption, all diseases are offensive in the sight of God' (ibid. p. 74; See also p. 74 and Parham, *Voice*, p. 50–1; *The Apostolic Faith*, vol. 1, no. 2, Oct. 1906, p. 1, col. 1; Nelson, pp. 190, 194, 213–14; Anderson, pp. 76, 99, 108–12.

Compare this with the statement of Carl Brumback who – in reference to the Azusa Mission and Parham's Stone's Folly building – claimed that 'the Pentecostal outpouring did not begin in a back alley mission but in a mansion!' (Brumback, Carl, *Suddenly from Heaven* [Springfield: Gospel Publishing House, 1977] p. 19).

12. Polman, G. R., Letter to G. A. Wumkers, 27 Feb. 1915 (trans. by P. N. van der Laan and Maryke Brevet). See also Wumkers, G. A., *De Pinksterbeweging Woornamelyk in Nederland* (Amsterdam, 1917) p. 4; (originally published as a leaflet in 1916) in which Wumkers virtually quotes Polman and notes that 'Because of that one also speaks of the Los Angeles-movement' (photostats provided by P. N. van der Laan, Apr. 1984).

13. See note 12.

14. See note 12.

15. Hollenweger, *Pentecostals*, pp. 223–55.

16. Anderson, Robert, *Spirit Manifestations and the Gift of Tongues*, 1912, in the catalogue of the British Library, vol. 8, pp. 67–8.

17. Synanm *Holiness–Pentecostal*, p. 109.

18. Ibid., p. 165.

19. Anderson, *Pentecostal*, p. 255. This is not so true of Britain where the Pentecostal movement tended to be working class but with some middle class leadership.

20. Nelson, p. 201.

21. Ibid., p. 201.

22. Synan, *Holiness–Pentecostal*, p. 168.

23. Lovett, p. 135.

24. Nelson, p. 203.

25. Ibid., p. 130; Bartleman, p. 54; Lovett, p. 136; Synan, Holiness–Pentecostal, p. 168.

26. Synan, *Holiness–Pentecostal* p. 177. See also Bloch-Hoell, pp. 173–4, who, however has a very limited understanding of what he describes as Pentecostal 'emotion' and 'ecstatic manifestations'.

27. Nelson, p. 202.

28. Washington, Joseph R., *Black Sects and Cults* (Garden City, New York: Anchor Press/Doubleday, 1973) *passim*.

29. Anderson, p. 102.

30. Christenson, Larry, 'Pentecostalism's Forgotten Forerunner' in Synan, *Aspects*, p. 72. Parham had also stressed the power aspect of Spirit baptism. He preached: 'The mighty power of God is just as capable in our lives today of performing His divine will as it was 1900 years ago. . . . The power of Pentecost is manifest in us. It has not been manifest in men for 1900 years, because the church has left the power of God. The Christian religion must be demonstrated. The world wants to be shown. Then let God's power be manifest thru us' (Parham, *Life*, p. 74; see also pp. 76, 113; Parham, Charles Fox, *A Voice Crying in the Wilderness* [Joplin,

Missouri: Joplin Printing Co., 1944; originally 1902] p. 4).

Parham's concept of spiritual power appears to have been mainly limited to glossolalia, divine healing and exorcism, Seymour, on the other hand, believed that the realities of a racist society and segregated church could also be transformed by the power of the Spirit.

31. Christenson, p. 72.
32. *The Apostolic Faith*, vol. 1, no. 1, Sept. 1906, p. 3, col. 2.
33. Ibid., vol. 1, no. 4, Dec. 1906, p. 1, col. 2.
34. Ibid., vol. 1, no. 1, Sept. 1906, p. 1, col. 3; p. 3, col. 3; no. 4, Dec. 1906, p. 1, col. 3 *passim*.
35. Ibid., vol. 1, no. 12, Jan. 1908, p. 2.
36. Lovett, p. 140.
37. Brunner, Emil, *The Misunderstanding of the Church* (London: Lutterworth Press, 1954) pp. 51–2.
38. Zegwaart, Hubert speaking at the Conference on Pentecostal and Charasmatic Research, University of Birmingham, Apr. 1984.
39. Just as the Holy Spirit in the Old Testament may be feminine, so also the Supreme Deity in West Africa often has maternal characteristics.

    Parham maintained that the Spirit should be controlled, while Seymour stressed that the Spirit should be in control. Parham, *Everlasting Gospel*, p. 66.
40. Lovett, p. 140. Previously quoted in Chapter 6 of this work.

    The Apostolic or Oneness Pentecostals have produced the rudiments of an original Pentecostal pneumatology and hence have retained more of the original dynamism than their trinitarian co-religionists. See Chapter 6, n42.
41. Synan, *Holiness–Pentecostal*, pp. 165–6, 178.
42. Synan, Ibid., pp. 179–80. See also Bloch-Hoell, p. 60.
43. Lovett, p. 139.
44. Synan, *Holiness–Pentecostal*, p. 114.
45. Parham, *Life*, p. 36.
46. Nelson, p. 3.
47. Lovett, pp. 127, 130–1.

CHAPTER 8: THE SPIRIT AND THE WALL

1. Hollenweger, Walter J. 'All Creatures Great and Small: Towards a Pneumatology of Life' in Martin, David and Mullen, Peter (eds), *Strange Gifts?: a Guide to Charasmatic Renewal* (Oxford: Basil Blockwell, 1984) pp. 41–3.
2. R. S. Rattray, writing of the Ashanti belief in God, claims that:
    In a sense ... it is true that this great Supreme Being, the conception of whom has been innate in the minds of the Ashanti, is the Jehovah of the Israelites. It was He who of old left His own dwelling above the vaulted sky, and entered the tent of dyed skins, when He came down to protect the Children of Israel in their march to the Promised Land. Rattray, Robert Sutherland, *Ashanti* (London: Greenwood Press, 1923) p. 141

While not necessarily agreeing with Rattray or seeking to identify African spirit possession with the baptism of the Holy Spirit, the acknowledgement of the presence of the Ruach Yahweh in pre-Christian Africa, opens up the possibility for a new understanding of African religion and of its relationship to Judaism and Christianity.

3. 1 Corinthians 1:4–7. See also 1 Kings 22:19ff.

4. 1 Samuel 16:14–23; 18:10; 19:9; 1 Kings 22:19–24; 2 Chronicles 18:19–23 and perhaps Judges 9:23.

5. Revelation 3:1; 4:5; 5:6. See also Revelation 1:4.

6. I have overheard elderly Jamaican Pentecostal women speaking of members of rival Pentecostal sects as 'praying against' the success of their congregation while they 'pray for it'. Some also believe that disaster can be prayed upon them by others.

7. 1 Corinthians 14:32, 40; 1 Thessalonians 5:19.

Bibliography

Sources prefaced with an * are quoted or cited indirectly.

Anderson, Robert Mapes, *A Social History of the Early Twentieth Century Pentecostal Movement*, Columbia University, PhD Thesis, 1969, reproduced by University Microfilms, High Wycombe, 1972. Also published in a revised form as *Vision of the Disinherited: the Making of American Pentecostalism* (New York: Oxford University Press, 1979).

Anderson, Robert, *Spirit Manifestations and the Gift of Tongues* (1912) in the catalogue of the British Library, vol. 8, pp. 67, 68.

Andrews, Edward D., *The People Called Shakers: a Search for the Perfect Society* (New York: Oxford University Press, 1953).

'An Official Report of the Trials of Sundry Negroes charged with an attempt to raise an insurrection in the State of South-Carolina ... prepared and published at the request of the Court', Charleston, 1822, republished in Aptheker, *Documentary History*.

Aptheker, Herbert, *A Documentary History of the Negro People in the United States* (New York: Citadel Press, 1969).

Aptheker, Herbert, *American Negro Slave Revolts* (New York: International Publishers, 1978; originally 1943).

Arinze, Francis A., *Sacrifice in Ibo Religion* (Ibadan, Nigeria: Ibadan University Press, 1970).

Armstrong, Herbert W., *The United States and British Commonwealth in Prophecy* (Pasadena, California: Ambassador College Press, 1972).

Awolalu, J. Omosade, *Yoruba Beliefs and Sacrificial Rites* (London: Longman, 1979).

*Barratt, T. B., *Urkristendommen* in Bloch-Hoell.

Barratt, David B., 'AD 2000:350 Million Christians in Africa' in *International Review of Mission*, vol. 59, no. 233, Jan. 1970, pp. 39–54.

Barratt, David B. (ed.), *World Christian Encyclopedia* (Oxford University Press, 1982).

Barth, Karl, *Church Dogmatics*, (trans. Bromley, G. W. and Torrance, T. F.), vol. 1 (Edinburgh: T and T Clark, 1975).

Bartleman, Frank, *Azusa Street* (originally entitled *How 'Pentecost' Came to Los Angeles – How It Was in the Beginning*), Plainfield, NJ: Logos International, 1980; originally 1925).

Bascom, William, 'Folk Lore and Literature' in Lystad.

Bascom, William, *Ifa Divination: Communication Between Gods and Men in West Africa* (Bloomington: Indiana University Press, 1969).

Bastide, Roger, *African Civilisations in the New World* (trans. Peter Green), (London: C. Hurst & Co., 1971; originally *Les Ameriques Noirs*, Paris: Editions Payot, 1967).

Beckmann, David M., 'Black Indigenous Churches' in *Afro-American Studies*, vol. 3, 1975.

Beckmann, David M., *Black Origins of Possession by the Holy Spirit*, unpublished paper, 1973.

131

Beckmann, David M., 'Trance from Africa to Pentecostalism' in *Concordia Theological Monthly*, vol. 45, no. 1, Jan. 1974.

Beier, Ulli, *The Return of the Gods: the Sacred Art of Susanne Wegner* (Cambridge University Press, 1975).

Bloch-Hoell, Nils, *The Pentecostal Movement* (Oslo: Universitetsforlaget; London: Allen & Unwin, 1964).

Blyden, Edward W., *Liberia's Offering* (New York: John A. Gray, 1862).

Braithwaite, Edward Kamau, *The Folk Culture of the Slaves in Jamaica* (London: New Beacon Books, 1981).

Brown, J. A. C., *Techniques of Persuasion: from Propaganda to Brainwashing* (Middx: Penguin Books, 1975; originally 1963).

Brumback, Carl, *Suddenly From Heaven* (Springfield: Gospel Publishing House, 1977).

Bruner, Frederick Dale, *A Theology of the Holy Spirit* (London: Hodder & Stoughton, 1970).

Brunner, Emil, *The Misunderstanding of the Church* (London: Lutterworth Press, 1954).

Bucher, Herbert, *Spirits and Power* (Cape Town: Oxford University Press, 1980).

Caldecott, Alfred, *The Church in the West Indies* (London: Frank Cass, 1970; originally 1898).

Campbell, David, 'Baptism in Two Elements' in *Pentecostal Truth*, vol. 1, no. 8, June 1973.

Carlisle, Rodney, *The Roots of Black Nationalism* (Port Washington, NY: National University Publications, 1975).

Church of God Evangel, published by The Church of God, Cleveland.

Chreitzberg, A. M., *Early Methodism in the Carolinas* (Nashville, Tennessee: np, 1897).

Christenson, Larry, 'Pentecostalism's Forgotten Forerunner' in Synan, *Aspects*.

Clanton, Arthur L., *United We Stand* (Hazelwood, Missouri: Pentecostal Publishing House, 1970).

Cone, James H., *The Spirituals and the Blues: an Interpretation* (New York: The Seabury Press, 1972).

Confidence, June, 1911.

Conn, Charles W., *Like a Mighty Army: a History of the Church of God* (Cleveland: Pathway Press, 1977).

*Cross, Witney R., *The Burned Over District* (New York: Harper & Row, 1965).

Currie, S. D., 'Speaking in Tongues: Early Evidence Outside the New Testament Bearing on Glossais Lalein' in *Interpretation*, 19 July 1965.

Cutten, George Barton, *Speaking with Tongues: Historically and Psychologically Considered* (New Haven, Conn.: Yale University Press, 1927).

Davenport, Frederick Morgan, *Primitive Traits in Religious Revivals* (New York: MacMillan, 1977).

Davies, John Gordon (ed.), *A Dictionary of Liturgy and Worship* (London: SCM Press, 1972).

Dayton, Donald W., 'Christian Perfection to the Baptism of the Holy Ghost' in Synan, *Aspects*.

Dieter, Melvin E., 'Wesleyan–Holiness Aspects of Pentecostal Origins' in Synan, *Aspects*.

Dorson, Richard M., *American Folk Lore* (University of Chicago Press, 1959).

Dorson, Richard M., *American Negro Folk Tales* (Greenwich, Conn.: Fawcett Publications, 1967).

Dugger, Lillie, *A. J. Tomlinson* (Cleveland, Tennessee: White Wing Publishing House, 1964).

Drummond, Andrew L., *Edward Irving and His Circle* (London: James Clark & Co., 1935).

DuBois, W. E. Burghardt, *The Negro* (London: Oxford University Press, 1970; originally 1915).

DuBois, W. E. Burghardt, *The Negro Church* (Atlanta University Press, 1903).

DuBois, W. E. Burghardt, *The Souls of Black Folks* (New York: Aaron Books, 1965).

Eggleston, Edward, *The Circuit Rider: a Tale of the Heroic Age* (New York: Charles Scribner's Sons, 1909).

Elim Evangel, published by the Elim Pentecostal Church in Britain.

Epega, Daniel Olarimwa, *The Basis of Yoruba Religion* (Nigeria: Ijamido Printers, 1971).

Ewart, Frank J., *The Phenomenon of Pentecost* (St. Louis: Pentecostal Publishing House, 1947).

Foster, Fred J., *Think It not Strange: a History of the Oneness Movement* (St. Louis: Pentecostal Publishing House, 1965).

Frazier, E. Franklin, *The Negro Church in America* (New York: Schocken Books, 1974; originally 1964).

Gaba, Christian R., *Scriptures of an African People: Ritual Utterances of the Anlo* (New York: Nok Publishers, 1973).

Gee, Donald, *The Pentecostal Movement* (London: Elim Publishing Co., 1949).

Genovese, Eugene D., *Roll Jordan Roll: the World the Slaves Made* (New York: Pantheon, 1972).

Gerloff, Roswith I. H., 'Blackness and Oneness (Apostolic) Theology: Crosscultural Aspects of a Movement' in Gill.

Golder, Morris E., *History of the Pentecostal Assemblies of the World* (Indianapolis, Ind.: Pentecostal Assemblies of the World, 1973).

Gill, Jeffrey H. (ed.), *Papers Presented to the First Occasional Symposium on Aspects of The Oneness Pentecostal Movement* (Cambridge, Mass.: Harvard Divinity School, 5–7 July, 1984).

Gray, Thomas R. (ed.), *The Confessions of Nat Turner, the Leader of the Late Insurrection in Southampton*, Baltimore, 1831, partly republished in Aptheker, *Documentary History*.

Gromaki, Robert G., *The Modern Tongues Movement* (NJ: Presbyterian and Reformed Publishing Co., 1972).

Hamilton, Charles V., *The Black Preacher in America* (New York: William Morrow and Co., 1972).

Hannan, Dennis, and Aldersmith, H., *British Israel Truth* (London, The Covenant Publishing Co., 1926).

Haskins, James, *Witchcraft, Mysticism and Magic in the Black World* (Garden City, NY: Doubleday and Co., 1974).

*Haywood, G. T., *A Voice Crying in the Wilderness*, vol. 2., no. 9., 1921.

Henke, Frederic G., 'The Gift of Tongues and Related Phenomena at the

Present Day' in *American Journal of Theology*, vol. XIII, 1909, pp. 196, 197.

Herskovits, Melville J., *The Myth of the Negro Past* (Boston: Beacon Press, 1958).

Hollenweger, Walter J., 'After Twenty Years' Research on Pentecostalism' in *Theology*, vol. LXXXVII, no. 720, Nov. 1982.

Hollenweger, Walter J., 'A Black Pentecostal Concept: A Forgotten Chapter of Black History: the Black Pentecostals' Contribution to The Church Universal' in *Concept*, no. 50, June 1970.

Hollenweger, Walter J., 'All Creatures Great and Small: towards a Pneumatology of Life' in Martin and Mullen.

Hollenweger, Walter J., *Pentecost Between Black and White: Five Cast Studies on Pentecost and Politics* (Belfast: Christian Journals, 1974).

Hollenweger, Walter J., *The Pentecostals* (London: SCM Press, 1972 (translated from the German *Enthusiastisches Christentum: die Pfings Tbewegung in Geschichte und Gegenwart*, Zurich, 1969)).

Hollenweger, Walter J., 'Spirituals' in Davies.

The Holy Bible (Hazelwood, Missouri: Word Aflame Press, 1973).

Idowu, E. Bolaji, *African Traditional Religion: a Definition* (London: SCM Press, 1973).

'Incidents in the Life of the Rev. J. Asher, Pastor of Shiloh (Coloured) Baptist Church, Philadelphia, United States, and a concluding chapter of facts illustrating the unrighteous prejudice existing in the minds of American citizens toward their coloured brethren', London, 1850, republished in Aptheker, *Documentary History*.

Isichei, Elizabeth (ed.), *Varieties of Christian Experience in Nigeria* (London: The MacMillan Press, 1982).

Jackson, Thomas (ed.), *The Works of John Wesley* (Grand Rapids, Michigan: Zondervan, 1959).

Johnson, F. Roy, *The Nat Turner Slave Insurrection* (Murfreesbro, NC: Johnson Publishing Co., 1966).

Johnson, F. Roy, *The Nat Turner Story* (Murfreesbro, NC: Johnson Publishing Co., 1970).

*Jones, Charles Colcock, *The Religious Instruction of Negroes in the United States* (Savannah: T. Porse Co., 1842).

Kansas City Journal, 22 Jan. 1901.

Kelsey, Morton T., *Tongues Speaking: an Experiment in Spiritual Experience* (London: Hodder & Stoughton, 1968).

*Kidson, W. E., *The Apostolic Herald*, July 1930.

Knox, Ronald A., *Enthusiasm: a Chapter in Religion with Special Reference to the 17th and 18th Centuries* (NY: Oxford University Press, 1961).

Kuiper, B. K., *The Church in History* (Grand Rapids: William B. Eerdmans Publishing Co., 1951).

Ladd, George Eldon, *The Presence of the Future* (London: SPCK, 1980), (originally *Jesus and the Kingdom*, NY: Harper & Row, 1964).

Lanternari, Vittorio, *The Religions of the Oppressed: a Study of Modern Messianic Cults*, (trans. Sergio, Lisa), (London: Macgibbon & Kee, 1963).

*Lietzmann, Hans, *The Founding of the Church Universal* (New York: Meridin Books, 1963).

Los Angeles Daily Times, Wednesday morning, 18 April 1906.

*Loud, Grover C., *Evangelised America* (NY: Dial Press, 1928).

Lovett, Leonard, 'Black Origins of the Pentecostal Movement' in Synan, *Aspects*.

Lovett, Leonard, 'Perspectives on the Black Origins of the Contemporary Pentecostal Movement', in *the Journal of the Interdenominational Theological Center*, vol. 1, 1973, pp. 42–6.

Lynch, Hollis R., *Black Spokesman: Selected Published Writings of Edward Wilmott Blyden* (London: Frank Cass, 1971).

Lynch, Hollis R., *Edward Wilmott Blyden, Pan-Negro Patriot, 1832–1912* (London: Oxford University Press, 1967).

Lystad, Robert A. (ed.), *The African World: a Survey of Social Research* (London: Pall Mall Press for African Studies Association, 1965).

*McClain, S. C., *Unpublished Notes*, in Clanton and Foster.

McLoughlin, William G., *Modern Revivalism: Charles Grandison Finney to Billy Graham* (New York: Ronald, 1959).

Martin, David and Mullen, Peter (eds), *Strange Gifts?: a Guide to Charistmatic Renewal* (Oxford: Basil Blockwell, 1984).

*May, Henry F., *Protestant Churches and Industrial America* (NY: Harper & Bros, 1949).

May, L. Carlyle, 'A Survey of Glossolalia and Related Phenomena in Non-Christian Religions' in *American Anthropologist*, vol. 58, 1956, pp. 75–96.

Mbiti, John S., *African Religions and Philosophy* (London: Heinemann, 1969).

Mbiti, John S., *Concepts of God in Africa* (London: SPCK, 1969).

Mbiti, John S., *Introduction to African Religion* (London: Heinemann, 1975).

Mbiti, John S., *New Testament Eschatology in an African Background: a Study of the Encounter Between New Testament Theology and African Traditional Concepts* (London: SPCK, 1978; originally 1971).

Meier, August and Rudwick, Elliot, *The Making of Black America* (NY: Atheneum, 1969).

Menzies, William W., 'Non-Wesleyan Origins of the Pentecostal Movement' in Synan, *Aspects*.

Mirinda, Osmundo Ofonso, *Apocalyptico-Eschatological Hope, the Theology of the Oppressed; an Enquiry into some Aspects of Popular Black Religion*, unpublished paper, Tuscaloosa, Alabama: Stillman College, 1971.

*Murphy, Jeanette Robinson, 'The Survival of African Music in America' on *Popular Science Monthly*, NY, 1899, no. 55.

Mullins, G. W., *Flight and Rebellion: Slave Resistance in Eighteenth Century Virginia* (New York: Oxford University Press, 1972).

Manuwal, Lewis, *Water Baptism According to the Bible and Historical References* (Hazelwood, Missouri: End-Time Ministries, nd).

Merriam, Allen, P., 'Music and Dance' in Lystad.

Metuh, Emefie Ikenga, *God and Man in African Religion* (London: Geoffrey Chapman/Cassell, 1981).

Minute Book of the Pentecostal Assemblies of the World, Inc. np (P A of W), 1981.

Minutes of the 51st General Assembly (Cleveland, Tennessee: Church of God, 1966).

Neibuhr, Richard H., *The Social Sources of Denominationalism* (NY: Living Age Books, 1957; originally 1929).

Nelson, Douglas J., *For Such a Time as This: the Story of Bishop William J. Seymour and the Azusa Street Revival*, unpublished PhD dissertation, University of Birmingham, May 1981.

Nickel, Thomas R., *The Amazing Shakarian Story* (Los Angeles: Full Gospel Business Men's Fellowship International, 1964).

*O'Dea, Thomas F., *The Mormons* (University of Chicago Press, 1957).

*Olmsted, Frederick Law, *The Cotton Kingdom*, vol. 1 (NY, 1861).

Parham, Sarah E. (comp.), *The Life of Charles F. Parham: Founder of the Apostolic Faith Movement* (Joplin, Missouri: Tri-State Printing Co., 1930).

*Parham, Charles Fox, *Apostolic Faith* (Baxter Springs, Kansas, Apr. 1925).

Parham, Charles Fox, *A Voice Crying in the Wilderness* (Joplin, Missouri: Joplin Printing Co., 1944; originally 1902).

Parham, Charles Fox, *The Everlasting Gospel* (Baxter Springs, Kansas, 1942).

Parrinder, Geoffrey 'The African Spiritual Universe' in Gates.

*Payne, Daniel Alexander, *Recollections of Seventy Years* (NY: Arno Press, 1969; originally 1886).

*Payne, Daniel Alexander, *History of the African Methodist Episcopal Church* (Nashville: Book Concern of the AME Church, 1891).

Pentecostal Truth, vol. I, no. 8, June 1973, published by United Pentecostal Church in Great Britain and Northern Ireland.

Polman, G. R. Letter to G. A. Wumkers, 27 Feb. 1915 (trans. by P. N. van der Laan and Maryke Brevet).

*Powdermaker, Hortense, *After Freedom* (NY: Atheneum, 1969).

*Quarles, Benjamin, *The Negro in the Making of America* (NY: Collier, 1964).

Raboteau, Albert J., *Slave Religion: the Invisible Institution in the Antebellum South* (Oxford University Press, 1978).

Rattray, Robert Sutherland, *Ashanti* (London: Greenwood Press, 1923).

*Redkey, Edwin S., *Black Exodus* (New Haven, Conn.: Yale University Press, 1969).

Reed, David Arthur, *Origins and Developments of the Theology of Oneness Pentecostalism in the US*, unpublished PhD Dissertation, Boston University, 1978.

Reed, David Arthur, *Aspects of the Origins of Oneness Pentecostalism* in Synan, *Aspects*.

Ssmarin, W. J., *Tongues of Men and Angels* (Toronto: Collier-Macmillan, 1972).

Savannah Unit, Georgia Writers' Project, *Drums and Shadows* (University of Georgia Press, 1960).

Schleiermacher, Friedrich D. E., *The Christian Faith* (English trans. of the second German edition), (Edinburgh: T. & T. Clarke, 1968).

*Seeberg, Reinhold, *Text-book of the History of Doctrines* (trans. Hay, Charles E.), (Grand Rapids, Michigan: Baker Book House, 1956).

*Seymour, William Joseph, *Amended Articles of Incorporation*, 19 May 1914.

Seymour, William Joseph, *The Apostolic Faith*, Los Angeles, California, Sept. 1906 to May 1908 (Republished as *Like As Of Fire*, Corum, Fred T., Wilmington Mass., 1981).

Shaw, E., *The Catholic Apostolic Church* (NY: King's Crown Press, 1946).

Simpson, George Eaton, *Black Religions in the New World* (NY: Columbia University Press, 1978).

Stone, James, *The Church of God of Prophecy, History and Polity* (Cleveland: White Wing Publishing House and Press, 1977).

Strachan, Gordon, *The Pentecostal Theology of Edward Irving* (London: Darton, Longmann & Todd, 1973).

Sunkler, Bengt, G. M., *Bantu Prophets in South Africa* (Oxford University Press for the International African Institute, 1961; originally Lutterworth Press 1948).

Sweetman, David, *Women Leaders in African History* (London: Heinemann Educational, 1984).

Synan, Vinson, (ed.), *Aspects of Pentecostal–Charasmatic Origins* (Plainfield, NJ: Logos International, 1975).

Synan, Vinson, *The Holiness–Pentecostal Movement in the United States* (Grand Rapids, Michigan: William B. Eerdmans Publishing Co., 1961).

Tinney James S. 'Black Origins of the Pentecostal Movement' in *Christianity Today*, 8 Oct. 1971.

Tinney, James S., *Competing Theories of Historical Origins for Black Pentecostalism*, paper presented at the Annual Meeting of the American Academy of Religion, 16 Nov., 1979 New York City.

Tinney, James S., 'The Significance of Race in the Rise and Development of the Apostolic Pentecostal Movement' in Gill.

Tinney, James S., 'William J. Seymour: Father of Modern Day Pentecostalism' in the *Journal of the Interdenominational Theological Center* Atlanta, Georgia, vol. 4, 1976, pp. 34–44.

*Tomlinson, A. J., *Journal of Happenings*, manuscript diary in the archives of the Church of God, Cleveland, Tennessee, 1901 to 1923.

*Tomlinson, A. J., *The Last Great Conflict* (Cleveland, Tennessee: Press of Walter E. Rodgers, 1913).

Tomlinson, A. J., *Minutes of the Sixteenth Assembly* (Cleveland, Tennessee, 1926).

Tomlinson, Homer A. (ed.), *Diary of A. J. Tomlinson* (NY: Church of God World Headquarters, 1945 to 1955, vols 1 and 3.

*Torrey, Reuben A., *The Baptism with the Holy Spirit* (NY: Flemming H. Ravell, 1895).

Van Dusen, Henry Pit, 'Caribbean Holiday' in *The Christian Century*, 17 Aug. 1955, p. 948.

Van Dusen, Henry Pit, 'Montana Indians and Pentecostals', in *The Christian Century*, 23 July 1958, p. 850.

Van Dusen, Henry Pit, 'The Third Force in Christendom', in *Life*, 9 June, 1958, p. 13.

Walker, David, 'Walker's Appeal in Four Articles: Together with a Preamble to the Colored Citizens of the World, but in particular, and very expressly to those in the United States of America', Boston, Massachusetts, 28 Sept. 1829, republished in Aptheker, *Documentary History*.

Washington, Booker T. and DuBois, W. E. B., *The Negro in the South* (NY: The Citadel Press, 1970; originally the William Levi Bull Lectures for 1907).

Washington, Joseph R., *Black Sects and Cults* (Garden City, NY: Anchor Press/ Doubleday, 1973).

Wesley, John, *A Plain Account of Christian Perfection* (London: The Epworth Press, 1976).

What We Believe and Teach: Articles of Faith of the United Pentecostal Church (St Louis, Missouri, nd).

White, Alma, *Demons and Tongues* (Zarephath, NJ: Pillar of Fire, 1951; originally 1902).

Williams, Brian, *Britain's Royal Throne* (Birmingham: Brian Williams Evangelistic Association, 1968).

Williams, Cyril G., *Tongues of the Spirit* (Cardiff: University of Wales Press, 1981).

Williams, Joseph, J., *Psychic Phenomena of Jamaica* (Westport, Conn.: Greenwood Press, 1979; originally NY: Dial Press , 1934).

Wilmore, Gayroud, S., *Black Religion and Black Radicalism* (New York: Doubleday & Co., 1972).

*Woodworth-Etter, Harry B., *Signs and Wonders God Wrought in the Ministry for Forty Years* (Chicago: the author, 1916).

Wumbkers, G. A., *De Pinksterbeweging Woornamelyk in Nederland* (Amsterdam, 1917).

Yetman, Norman R., *Voices from Slavery* (NY: Holt Reinhart & Winston, 1970).

Zikmund, Barbara Brown, *Asa Mahn and Oberlin Perfectionism*, PhD thesis, Duke University, 1969, reproduced by University Microfilms, 1970.

Index

CPSIA information can be obtained
at www.ICGtesting.com
Printed in the USA
LVHW101255210123
737603LV00006B/292